796.01

KT-367-990

Sport and Character

Reclaiming the Principles of Sportsmanship

10.72

Craig Clifford

Randolph M. Feezell

Human Kinetics

Withdrawn

TO5b942

796.01

Library of Congress Cataloging-in-Publication Data

Clifford, Craig Edward, 1951-
  Sport and character: reclaiming the principles of sportsmanship / Craig Clifford and Randolph M. Feezell.
    p. cm.
  Includes bibliographical references.
  ISBN-13: 978-0-7360-8192-4 (soft cover)
  ISBN-10: 0-7360-8192-5 (soft cover)
  1. Sportsmanship. I. Feezell, Randolph M., 1950- II. Title.
  GV706.3.C56 2010
  174'.9796--dc22

                              2009025544

ISBN-10: 0-7360-8192-5 (print)   ISBN-10: 0-7360-8609-9 (Adobe PDF)
ISBN-13: 978-0-7360-8192-4 (print)   ISBN-13: 978-0-7360-8609-7 (Adobe PDF)

Copyright © 2010 by Human Kinetics, Inc.

All rights reserved. Except for use in a review, the reproduction or utilization of this work in any form or by any electronic, mechanical, or other means, now known or hereafter invented, including xerography, photocopying, and recording, and in any information storage and retrieval system, is forbidden without the written permission of the publisher.

This book is a revised edition of *Coaching for Character,* published in 1997 by Human Kinetics, Inc.

Acquisitions Editor: Jenny Maddox Abbott; **Developmental Editor:** Laura Floch; **Assistant Editor:** Laura Podeschi; **Copyeditor:** Alisha Jeddeloh; **Proofreader:** Kathy Bennett; **Permission Manager:** Martha Gullo; **Graphic Designer:** Nancy Rasmus; **Graphic Artist:** Julie L. Denzer; **Cover Designer:** Keith Blomberg; **Photographer (cover):** Christof Koepsel/Bongarts/Getty Images; **Photographer (interior):** Human Kinetics, unless otherwise noted; **Photo Asset Manager:** Laura Fitch; **Photo Production Manager:** Jason Allen; **Printer:** Versa Press

Copies of this book are available at special discounts for bulk purchase for sales promotions, premiums, fund-raising, or educational use. Special editions or book excerpts can also be created to specifications. For details, contact the Special Sales Manager at Human Kinetics.

Printed in the United States of America   10   9   8   7   6   5   4   3   2   1

The paper in this book is certified under a sustainable forestry program.

Human Kinetics
Web site: www.HumanKinetics.com

United States: Human Kinetics
P.O. Box 5076
Champaign, IL 61825-5076
800-747-4457
e-mail: humank@hkusa.com

Canada: Human Kinetics
475 Devonshire Road Unit 100
Windsor, ON N8Y 2L5
800-465-7301 (in Canada only)
e-mail: info@hkcanada.com

Europe: Human Kinetics
107 Bradford Road
Stanningley
Leeds LS28 6AT, United Kingdom
+44 (0) 113 255 5665
e-mail: hk@hkeurope.com

Australia: Human Kinetics
57A Price Avenue
Lower Mitcham, South Australia 5062
08 8372 0999
e-mail: info@hkaustralia.com

New Zealand: Human Kinetics
Division of Sports Distributors NZ Ltd.
P.O. Box 300 226 Albany
North Shore City
Auckland
0064 9 448 1207
e-mail: info@humankinetics.co.nz

E4775

Sport and Character

Reclaiming the Principles of Sportsmanship

CONTENTS

PREFACE

It seemed inevitable that we would write this book. Anytime we talked, the conversation would turn to the topic of sport—and then, inevitably, to sportsmanship. We talked about trying to teach it to the kids we were coaching and the kids we were raising; we talked about watching its occasional display and its frequent absence in college and professional athletics. Expressions such as "respect for the game," "respect for the opponent," and "respect for officials" repeatedly surfaced. We apologized to each other for invoking sportsmanship clichés in our conversations, until one day we realized that expressions which sound like clichés to us many young athletes today have never heard.

In 1985, Gerald Ford remarked,

> *Broadly speaking, outside of a national character and an educated society, there are few things more important to a country's growth and well-being than competitive athletics. If it is a cliché to say athletics build character as well as muscle, then I subscribe to the cliché.*

A generation ago many people might have nodded approvingly when such views were expressed. Several decades later it is difficult to be as charitable when thinking about the moral possibilities of sport participation. What are our children learning as they turn off ESPN and hurry off to practice? There was a time when they may have had the good fortune of watching Mickey Mantle trot around the bases after hitting a home run, head down so as not to show up the opposing pitcher, exhibiting a respect for his opponents and humility and grace in relation to the traditions and reality of the game of baseball. Now what do they learn when they watch sports on TV? Respect for opponents? Humility? Grace? Loyalty? Hardly. It would be tedious to recite a lengthy list of the disturbing aspects of contemporary sport: bench-clearing brawls, trash talking, taunting, strutting, college athletic scandals, cheating, drug abuse—why go on?

A cover story by columnist Robert Lipsyte in the April 2, 1995, issue of the *New York Times Magazine* even proclaimed the end of American sport:

Sports are over because they no longer have any moral resonance. They are merely entertainment, the bread and circuses of a New Rome. Nothing makes this more chillingly real than our current Babes: Mike Tyson and Tonya Harding. Two of the neediest, hungriest, most troubled and misguided young people in athletic history, they are the archetypal extremes of this frenzied, confused sports endgame. (p. 56)

When we consider the years since Lipsyte's hyperbolic proclamation, it's hard to believe that things have improved in the world of sport. Some of the biggest news stories have continued to document these problems, despite pockets of resistance that have formed in various cultural venues: books about the importance (and decline) of moral character in society, character education programs in our schools, organizations devoted to promoting better behavior in sport, and so forth.

But merely bemoaning the situation is not enough. Something seems to have happened concerning the substance of our collective moral lives, in sport and in society at large—and some kind of response is called for. In such a contemporary context, we think our book on sportsmanship is important and timely. We can't expect children to do what is right if we don't teach them. We can't expect children to become good people unless we attempt to instill good habits in them and help them develop good character traits. Virtue, said Aristotle, requires practice. We contend that one can, and must, *practice* sportsmanship, just as one must practice a fast break, a baserunning situation, or the timing for a poach in tennis doubles. But we can't teach children sportsmanship and guide them in its practice if we don't know what it is or why it's important. Although many have bemoaned the situation in today's sports world, there appears to be little available in the way of a clear articulation of the basic principles of sportsmanship.

Given the overwhelming numbers of young people who are involved in sport as participants, spectators, and fans, it is imperative to reclaim moral language for sport in order for this part of their lives to be charged with the possibilities of moral growth and excellence of character. Sport is not the only arena, but it can and should be an important one for practicing virtue. And it doesn't just happen of its own accord. Sport can—and often does—inculcate the worst habits, the worst character. In 1962, Brutus Hamilton, the great track and field coach, said: "When ideals are obscured in amateur sports, then comes the danger of an athletic injury to the character of the athlete" (Walton, p. 117). One thing is sure: How we conduct ourselves as players, coaches, parents, and school administrators will make its mark upon the kinds of human beings we are going to be. Sport is an expression of our culture, and because of the enormous importance we attribute to it, it shapes that culture as well.

Being a good sport also requires proper perspective about what sporting activity is and what its central values are. In this sense, sportsmanship involves a kind of wisdom that requires proper insight, right attitudes, and good judgment, as well as appropriate conduct. Sport can and should teach lessons, and such lessons can be crucial for self-understanding. As you will see, we believe that sportsmanship primarily involves *respect:* for the opponent, for teammates, for officials, for coaches, and for the game. The principles of good sportsmanship do not supply specific rules for behavior; rather, they supply the general guidelines and the context in which good judgment, relying on experience and understanding, can arrive at specific decisions in a meaningful way. It is precisely that context that seems to be missing in today's sports culture.

The thread that runs through the entire book is a philosophic return to the old-fashioned notion of *sportsmanship* as the unifying moral concept that describes good character in sport. We chose the word as our central concept after much consideration and much discussion with coaches and ex-coaches who care about the sorts of things we are trying to express. As for it being old-fashioned, we need a word that carries the weight of tradition, for it is our contention that we need to get back in touch with something we were once in touch with. We also hasten to say that the second syllable of the word should not be taken to exclude female athletes; indeed, it's arguable that girls' and women's athletics have continued to place a far greater emphasis on sportsmanship than the male version. In its etymological origin, the word "man" is generic, and "sports-person-ship" or "sports-human-ship" would be an abomination of language that would send most athletes, male and female, scampering out of the locker room in hysterical laughter. We occasionally resort to the expression "being a good sport," but even that expression doesn't have the resonance of the traditional noun. In an informal survey, we found several women's basketball coaches, themselves women, who quite reasonably avoid the expression "man-to-man" defense but don't hesitate to use the term "sportsmanship." Our position is simple: Excellence of character, on the playing field and in life generally, is just as important for girls and women as it is for boys and men.

This book represents a reworking and expansion of an earlier publication, *Coaching for Character.* And much of what we have to say in *Sport and Character: Reclaiming the Principles of Sportsmanship* is addressed to coaches who work with young athletes. Part of the reason for the new title is that we want to indicate that this book, although some of it is explicitly addressed to coaches, has something to say to anyone who is interested in the issue of sportsmanship. Whether you are involved with the world of sport as a coach, an athlete, a parent, a teacher, a minister, a school administrator, or a citizen concerned about the social fabric of American culture, you face tough decisions about ethical matters, and many of these matters ultimately relate to your most basic views about the very nature of sport—why it's important to you, why you care about it, and how sport relates to other basic values.

While you can scarcely avoid the many situations in which you must make important ethical decisions, you can certainly avoid thoughtfully engaging these issues. This avoidance is what we want to challenge. We want to challenge you to become more reflective about athletic competition. We want you to think with us. You may not agree with everything we say, but that's natural. Our goal is not to preach, but to encourage and to help. We encourage you to think for yourself, and we challenge you to develop your own answers to these questions. However, we believe we can help you think about these issues and give you a framework within which you can make your own decisions and help your players grow not just as athletes but as human beings. The ultimate goal of ethical reflection is practical: It makes a difference in how you act, in how you treat others, and in what kind of person you are.

We hope this book will be useful as a basis for discussion and reflection about virtuous conduct in sport. We want this book to engage and provoke you, as well as guide and instruct. We believe that something good happens to people when they engage in dialogue and reflection about important human concerns. Long ago Socrates argued that we should be most concerned about virtue and the greatest possible care of our souls. He exhorted his fellow Athenians to try, above all, to make themselves as good and as wise as possible. Reading a book on sportsmanship and thinking about such issues may appear to be a trivial response to Socrates' challenge. Yet where else do we have such an opportunity to connect with young people in an area they care about and raise these questions again and again? Why not exhort young athletes to be as good and as wise as possible when they play their games, as well as in life as a whole?

CREDITS

Photo © Rich Clarkson/Sports Illustrated/Getty Images on page 8.

Photo © AP Photo/Amy Sancetta on page 20.

Photo © AP Photo/Peter Cosgrove on page 37.

Photo © AP Photos/Tom Mihalek on page 51.

Photo © John McDonough/Icon SMI on page 52.

Photo © Norbert Schmidt/Imago/Icon SMI on page 61.

Photo © Otto Gruele/Allsport/Getty Images Sport on page 73.

Photo © Tony Ding/Icon SMI on page 88.

Photo © Action Plus/Icon SMI on page 94.

Photo © TIM ZIELENBACH/AFP/Getty Images on page 104.

INTRODUCTION
Sport Today

The year was 1954 when the University of Oklahoma played Texas Christian University in the biggest college football game of the season up to that point. Oklahoma had won a national championship in 1950, and from 1953 until 1957 the team would win two more national championships and 47 games in a row. Oklahoma came into the game ranked number three in the country; TCU was ranked number four. You get the point: This was a huge game with a packed stadium and national attention. As the clock ran down in the fourth quarter with Oklahoma ahead, 21–16, TCU marched down the field and the quarterback threw an apparent touchdown pass into the end zone just before time ran out. The field judge signaled touchdown. The receiver walked toward the official, handed him the ball, and said, "Ref, I didn't catch it. I trapped it."

Hard to imagine. In this day and age, where receivers often are shown on the replay pretending to catch a ball that was trapped (and undoubtedly celebrating in some showy fashion)—or in baseball, where it happens all the time that an outfielder traps a ball and holds it up as if he made a legitimate catch—the receiver's behavior seems unreal, fictional, even absurd. Now return to the game. The back judge saw the trapped catch, had some uncertainty, and initially didn't want to overrule the field judge. They discussed the play, and because the receiver admitted that he didn't catch the ball cleanly, the original call was reversed. The result: incomplete pass, Oklahoma victory, and a rather amazing example of sportsmanship and fair play.

Can you imagine such behavior in a comparably significant big-time college football game today, for example, Ohio State versus Michigan, Florida versus Georgia, or Texas versus Oklahoma? If you find such behavior so unrealistic or improbable in the context of sport today, it might be worthwhile to wonder what has happened in sport, or better, whether some important change has occurred in our attitudes toward our games, our expectations and judgments about athletic events, and our emotional reactions to our team's wins and losses, our heroes' achievements and failures, our children's successes and defeats.

Fast forward to April 2008, and a less exalted sports venue, yet no less important for the players, coaches, and fans of two division II college softball teams vying for a conference championship. A senior part-time starter for Western Oregon steps to the plate with two runners on base and hits the first home run of her college career. As she's trying to retrace her steps after missing first base when she rounded the bag, her right knee gives out and she falls in a heap, unable to continue her home-run trot. The rules apparently allow no assistance from any other teammates or coaches, and permit only a pinch runner at first, the consequence of which is that a three-run homer would be reduced to a two-run single. A career highlight would be reduced to a humdrum occurrence. Central Washington's first baseman has a better idea. After consulting with the umpires, she and a teammate carry the injured player around the bases, stopping briefly at each one so she can lightly tap it with her left foot. At home plate the injured player is passed to her teammates. The Central Washington players return to their positions as the fans continue to cheer a remarkable display of sportsmanship. Is sportsmanship dead? No. Is it on life support? Probably not. Is there work to do? Yes, much work is required.

The national reaction to what was called "the ultimate act of sportsmanship," "an unforgettable story of compassion and selflessness amid intense competition," was "pretty phenomenal," said the sports information director from Western Oregon. Numerous media outlets around the country covered the story. We might wonder, however, why this act was taken to be so extraordinary. The very reaction seemed to say something about "our" assumptions concerning what kind of behavior we expect in the heat of "intense competition." Why would we think that attitudes toward competition, winning, and opponents would be such that helping an injured opponent would be trumpeted as an act of ethical heroism rather than a praiseworthy but expected action, hardly the stuff for ESPN highlights, effusive praise, and national applause? The TCU receiver played by the rules, and the Central Washington players helped an opponent achieve what she deserved, yet we are startled by these actions, which are so contrary to the single-minded pursuit of victory. Pam Knox, the Western Oregon coach, said this about the events that unfolded during the game: "It kept everything in perspective and the fact that we're never bigger than the game. . . . It was such a lesson that we learned—that it's not all about winning. And we forget that, because as coaches, we're always trying to get to the top. We forget that. But I will never, ever forget this moment. It's changed me, and I'm sure it's changed my players" (Hayes 2008).

Why do we forget? Why is this so difficult to remember? We may be less surprised by current events at the other end of the ethical spectrum. However memorable we find our favorite historical or relatively recent examples of ethically meritorious actions in sport—from Olympians who have sacrificed their medals to help overturn an opponent's unjust disqualification to tennis players, race car drivers, and soccer players who have sought to do the right thing rather than the expedient one—our contemporary discussions are often dominated by disheartening examples of cheating, disrespect, and even violence. The head coach of the most successful National Football League franchise since 2002 is involved in a cheating scandal in which an assistant was caught videotaping New York Jets defensive signals from the sidelines during a game. As a result, the NFL penalizes the New England Patriots and coach Bill Belichick $750,000 and a first-round draft pick for cheating. Former senator George Mitchell is named to lead an intensive investigation into the use of performance-enhancing drugs in Major League Baseball. In 2007, the Mitchell Report states that "for more than a decade there has been widespread use of steroids and other performance enhancing substances by players in Major League Baseball, in violation of federal law and baseball policy." In a memo to all Major

League Baseball players, Mitchell says, "The illegal use of performance enhancing substances is a serious violation of the rules of Major League Baseball which directly affects the integrity of the game. The principal victims are the majority of players who don't use such substances." Our heroes are paraded in front of congressional committees and are exposed, much to our disappointment. But everyone does it. Cyclists and track athletes are also found guilty, but they're just trying to win, aren't they? "If you ain't cheatin', you ain't tryin'," says the NASCAR fan. Isn't that what we expect from our coaches and athletes? Why be upset when they merely respond to the prevailing ethos of contemporary sport? It's all about winning, isn't it?

Despite outstanding examples of good ethical conduct in sport and increasing institutional interest in these issues across a wide range of organizations, it's difficult not to be pessimistic about the state of sport today in relation to the ideals of good sportsmanship. It's important, however, not to overstate the case. Such pessimism expresses our sense that the ethical climate of modern sport is at least ambivalent, sometimes even hostile to the notion that questions of good character and conduct are important notions that we must take seriously when we think about sport and athletics. One contemporary thinker, Simon Blackburn, asks us to become sensitive not only to our physical environment but also to our moral or ethical environment. This is the surrounding climate of ideas about how to live. It determines what we find acceptable or unacceptable, admirable or contemptible. It determines our conception of when things are going well and when they are going badly. It shapes our emotional responses, determining what is the cause of pride or shame, or anger or gratitude, and what can be forgiven and what cannot. It gives us our standards—our standards of behavior.

This notion provides a particularly useful way of engaging important issues. For example, as Blackburn points out, we tend to talk more about our rights than about what is good, as classical ethicists did in both Western and non-Western philosophy. We don't talk much about a life devoted to duty, as the Victorians might have. We value individualism and freedom. We don't like to be told what to do by supposed moral authorities. We think our privacy should be vigorously protected from governmental interference. Although we may take certain ethical ideals to be obvious or unchallengeable, it's important to think carefully about such ideas, to critically examine them and see whether they can survive important questions about their status and consequences.

We might distinguish the general set of surrounding ideas about how to live and the ethical atmosphere within which vital parts of life are located—sport, business, the professions, and so on. Of course, there will be interesting interactions between the general ethical climate and more localized ethical milieus. In chapter 1 when we consider some common objections to teaching sportsmanship, we may think that the skepticism about moralizing and moral authorities in sport represents a more general skepticism or relativism derived from our ethical surroundings. Now consider the ethical climate of sport today—that is, the surrounding ideas about what sport is, how participants should conduct themselves, what their proper motives should be, when things are going well or badly, and what should be the shape of our emotional responses to various involvements in sport. Let's try to identify, as best we can, what appears to be a predominant attitude toward sport, expressed in the language we use to talk about sport and athletes, as well as the most powerful metaphors that guide our experiences and underlie our expectations and standards of behavior. And if we find some tension between the ethical climate surrounding sport today and the principles that are central to sportsmanship, then it should not surprise us that we face an uphill battle—to use a very common sports metaphor—in "reclaiming the principles of sportsmanship."

Turn on ESPN. Tune in to sports talk radio. Go online. Read the sports page. What is sport? What are the dominant concepts and metaphors that express the ethical climate of contemporary sport? First, sport is about winning, period. If your team is bad, break the contract and demand to be traded so you can realize the holy grail—the championship. The athlete must achieve the championship, and it's ultimately important to be recognized, paradoxically, as the individual who is best, at least in team sports, because she earned the ring—with teammates. If it's all about winning, then one may as well cheat to win (notwithstanding the important notion that sports are constituted by rules, to play the game is to follow the rules, and to violate constitutive rules, that is, to cheat, seems to mean that the cheater can't really "win", since the cheater isn't really playing the game at all). If sport is just about winning, then becoming excellent, playing well, relating to others, engaging in meaningful activity, experiencing the joy of athletic competition—none of these really matter. Second place is un-American—the silver medal is for losers. What are the consequences for children, fans, coaches, and players if we accept the win-at-all-costs attitude?

Alongside the reductive notion that sport is simply about winning is the emphasis on sport as a competitive activity, a zero-sum game in which losing is the ultimate disgrace and your opponent wants to take something from you, even humiliate you. Metaphors associated with war reinforce the notion that athletes are warriors engaged in battle against an enemy. Trash talking and taunting are common behaviors against opponents. We're trying to kill our opponents. Let's murder, trounce, stomp, or destroy them. No doubt sport is competitive, but what's missing or downplayed is the cooperative aspect of sport in which participants come together not in war, but in an attempt to become excellent or simply to engage in interesting and satisfying activities in an artificially constructed arena of shared meanings and values. Are we surprised by the Central Washington players' actions because we don't expect altruism or benevolence on the field of battle? (After all, we're trying to "kill" the other team.) Are we expected to be indifferent or perhaps even unkind to our mortal enemies, especially if it enhances our chance at winning?

Next, for many, sport is entertainment, pure display offered for the pleasure of the spectators. (Ignore for the moment how limited such a view of sport is.) If sport is entertainment, then the athlete should do what is entertaining, and those who entertain best should be rewarded. The gaudy celebrations and choreographed displays after the touchdown, sack, dunk, or goal entertain, don't they? But they also reinforce the "look-at-me" attitude that sometimes degenerates into tawdry forms of self-indulgence, both on and off the field. So younger athletes may come to see themselves as future professional entertainers (or current "amateur" performers in big-time college athletics) characterized by selfishness, greed, and arrogance. Entitlement means that the sports world revolves around the star.

Sport is also viewed as big business, or simply motivated by the aspiration to become bigger, economically speaking. If "no one cares" about a sporting event because no one is watching, then no one is entertained and no one is paying for the seats. The ultimate put-down of an athletic event on sports talk radio is that "no one cares," as if the event's value is directly proportional to its ability to occasion fan interest, usually evaluated in terms of monetary power or television ratings. The path to success, at even lower levels of sport, is to build "The Program," improve the facilities in order to increase interest and keep the turnstiles moving. Fire the high school coach who can't survive this model, whose evaluation is intimately related to economic considerations. Bring in the illegal player and be sure to keep him eligible. Ignore bad attitudes for the sake of success. Forget about integrity and honor.

Sport is also about playing with emotion in an arena of intense competition. The blood-curdling screams after the "big play" may have once seemed like adolescent displays of lack of self-control. Now the big boys and girls are teaching the little boys and girls it's all right to scream, pump your fists, and beat your chest. Such displays are the norm at lower and lower levels of competitive sport. "Look what I've done! And, it's all about me!" Sport is supposedly about playing with passion, even if such emotion initiates disrespect for opponents, teammates and team, officials, and the game itself. Excuse or ignore the stupid displays that hurt a team's chances for victory because of penalties. That's just playing with emotion.

In part, the ethical climate that surrounds popular sports involves the following: Sport is about winning, competition, entertainment, market values, and highly emotional involvements. That's what we hear over and over about sport conducted at the highest levels, and the atmosphere that is created by such attitudes filters down into sport at all levels, in sometimes insidious ways. It's not that sport doesn't involve winning and competition and passionate commitment. It's not that sport doesn't inevitably involve economic matters. The problem is what is left out when we focus so much on these ethical ideas and their consequences. And make no mistake about it—these ideas are ethical in a broad sense, in just the way suggested by the notion of an "ethical climate" within which we develop our preferences, make our evaluative judgments, and shape our emotional responses. "Winning isn't everything, it's the only thing." "Show me a good loser and I'll show you a loser." "Losing is like death." "If winning is not the point, then why do they keep the score?" "Sport is about winning championships." They're clichés, of course, but they never seem to be extinguished. They are often embodied in the actions of coaches, athletes, and fans, and they form the foundation for standards of behavior that may come into conflict with the principles of sportsmanship—at least the ones we attempt to explain and defend in this book.

As we write this, the sports pages have included the following stories in the last few days: During a state 3A high school championship baseball game in Georgia,

BISHOP BURTON COLLEGE

a pitcher and catcher who are angry over the umpire's calls conspire to commit what would probably count as assault and battery if it happened outside the ballpark. The pitcher throws a high fastball. The catcher pretends he is expecting a low curveball and ducks. The ball hits the umpire in the facemask. Ten WNBA players and a coach are suspended and fined for a "dustup" in a women's professional basketball game. Members of the U.S. Olympic swim team are involved with accusations about endorsing products banned by the NCAA and positive drug tests. A local father is banned from Little League for a year because he assaulted an umpire after a baseball game played by 12-year-olds. And so it goes.

Examples are everywhere, some uplifting, others dismaying. To the extent that the ethical climate of sport today has something to do with the conduct that we fret about, it's appropriate to keep trying to counteract such influences. We hope our book continues to function in this way.

In part I, Thinking About Sportsmanship, we'll provide a foundation for the rest of the book. In part II, The Principles of Sportsmanship, we'll develop a series of principles that derive from the foundation we've laid down in part I. In part III, Thinking About Sport and Life, we'll ask you to go beyond the playing fields of athletic competition and think about sport in relation to the rest of life.

Some of the things we say in part I might seem somewhat abstract, but the principles of sportsmanship that we offer in part II—respect for opponents, for the team, for officials, for the game—must be based on *something*. Otherwise, they will float about as nothing more than groundless recommendations. We believe these principles of respect are not merely the subjective impressions of the authors. Ultimately, the principles of sportsmanship are grounded in the very nature of what we're about as players, coaches, and human beings. Thinking about sport, as we'll see in part III, will inevitably lead us to the most fundamental questions about life. So bear with us—and think with us. That beautiful jump shot you had in high school won't help you, but the tenacity and courage that you've developed in the heat of athletic competition will.

PART I

Thinking About Sportsmanship

ONE

The unexamined life is not worth living.

~ Plato, Apology of Socrates

Reflecting on Your Own Experience

EXPERIEI

VALUES REFLECTION EXPERIENCE

The best place to start this process is with your own experience. We will ask you to allow your own experience—and your understanding of it—to be challenged, but we won't ask you to leave that experience behind. Most of you probably already attempt to instill the values of sportsmanship in your players. But how important is it in your coaching? Do your players exhibit sportsmanlike behavior? Do you?

A Challenge to Reflect

Here are some questions that might help you reflect on your own experience. Write out your answers.

1. Who are the coaches I most respect? Why do I respect them? What qualities do they have that I most admire?
2. How do I want to be remembered by my athletes? How will they think of me later in life? Will I have made some difference in their lives? Will they want their children to play for me? To be like me?
3. Am I the kind of coach I would want my children to play for? If not, why?
4. Which of my former coaches do I most admire? Which of my former coaches do I least admire? Why?
5. Do I care most about being liked or about being respected by my players? Do my players like me? Respect me? Neither? Both?

What do your answers show you about your own coaching? What do they indicate about how serious you are about sportsmanship and character? These questions are meant to challenge you to look squarely at your own sense of what really matters to you as a coach.

Respect Starts With You

Following are the personal reflections of one current coach about his own past experience:

My American Legion baseball coach was one of the finest persons I've ever met. He never raised his voice. He was gentle but firm. I never saw him argue with an umpire. He treated every player with the utmost respect. He made us practice long and hard, but my impression was that all the players felt grateful to be coached by him. We all tried as hard as we could—for him. If you messed up, especially if you made a mental error, one little glance from him was enough to make you realize how much you had let him and the team down. He never allowed us to yell at other players or rag the umpires. And other coaches and teams knew this. I saw umpires apologize to him for making bad calls. He taught us the values of respect, responsibility, team play, and effort. It's really hard to put into words what he meant to all of us. I would have tried to run through a brick wall for him, and I know I'm a better person because I played for him.

Maybe we can't all be revered like this coach, but examples from your own experience probably show how much coaches can matter to players. Don't underestimate the extent to which players make judgments about their coaches. Because of your behavior, your players know that you approve of some things and disapprove of others. They know that you have certain values. What values are you conveying to your players? Answer the following questions honestly.

1. Do you allow your players to talk trash to opponents?
2. Do you allow your players to respond to an officiating call with angry displays of temper?
3. Do you let your players showboat, or prance, after they do something positive?
4. Do you ever yell or scream at players?
5. If you do yell or scream at players, do you do it when they perform poorly or when they behave in an unsportsmanlike manner?
6. Would you allow your team to depart after a game without shaking the opponents' hands?
7. Have you ever blamed a loss on an official (especially when talking to your players after the game)?
8. Have you ever made excuses for losing a game?
9. Would you attempt to intimidate an official in order to get a favorable call in the future?
10. Would you get into a heated argument with an official in order to motivate your team?
11. Would you promote animosity between two teammates to motivate them?
12. Would you run up the score on a team for any reason?
13. Do you ever call your players names in a way that demeans them or publicly embarrasses them?
14. Do you treat your players differently after a loss than after a win?
15. Do you punish or reward your players as a result of whether the team won or lost a match or game, without regard for the effort they put out?

Thinking About Reasons

Now take another step. Go back through the questions we just asked and ask yourself *why* you do or don't engage in these practices. If, for example, you do allow your players to talk trash to opponents, why? If you don't, why don't you? If you would run up the score on an opponent, why? If not, why not? And so on. Do you have good reasons for your answers? In other words, ask yourself not just what you do in your coaching but what you think you *should* be doing. Go back through each of the questions and ask yourself, regardless of what you actually do, whether you condone or condemn the practice. And then ask yourself what reasons you have for each judgment.

If you're willing to reflect on the reasons behind your actions and attitudes—which means that you're willing to risk the possibility of admitting you're wrong if your reasons don't hold up—then we think you'll find the following chapters helpful. We won't tell you exactly how you ought to answer these questions. We will, however, articulate a set of principles in light of which you ought to address these questions. These principles may challenge the way you've answered them—at the very least this should be an opportunity to become more reflective about what you do. Or you may very well come away from this book with the same answers to these questions but with a better understanding of the reasons behind your answers—and your actions.

Common Objections to Teaching Sportsmanship

We can imagine that some coaches might be skeptical about our emphasis on sportsmanship. It's not universally agreed that coaches have a responsibility to teach sportsmanship. Some of the objections are fairly prevalent, and we'd like to respond to them before we get under way.

Many coaches object to the call for sportsmanship because they see it as out-moded. Times have changed. Kids are different today, so you can't coach them the same way that we were coached when we were kids. Other successful coaches let their players trash-talk or vent their emotions, so why shouldn't I? I have to be in step with the times. You can't expect players today to act like monks or nuns. Why can't coaches let players be themselves?

Times may have changed, but in a very important sense, the sports we coach and play have not. Just because more people today, in sport and in society at large, act in disrespectful and uncivil ways doesn't mean that we must judge such actions as acceptable. Instead of throwing up our hands and saying kids are different so we must coach them differently, we should ask ourselves whether in fact they are different because we've coached them—and in general educated them—differently. It may be that because there is such an emphasis on winning and being "number one," we have forgotten the extent to which the language of sportsmanship has been central to the great athletic traditions. If unsportsmanlike behavior now seems to be the status quo, that doesn't mean that it has to be. It does mean that coaches have a huge responsibility to constantly teach, practice, and exemplify good sportsmanship. Someone must step forward and challenge the status quo. The truth of the matter is, sportsmanship doesn't restrict self-expression or require monkish behavior. There are good reasons for requiring players to be good sports, and people with good moral character are no less free to "express" themselves than are bad sports. They may simply do this differently.

The "times have changed" objection to sportsmanship in effect amounts to a form of historical relativism. Another prevalent objection to sportsmanship takes the form of a kind of cultural relativism. Values are relative to cultures, and many of the athletes today come out of urban cultures with values that are different from the mainstream values. In some cultures, outward displays of emotion are more acceptable. It's just a bunch of old white guys who've never been to the playground in the 'hood who criticize taunting and trash-talking.

Certainly, the principles of sportsmanship will get expressed in different ways because of differences of culture and personality. And coaches certainly need to have an appreciation for cultural differences. True, a cookie-cutter approach to molding character—expecting all athletes to behave in exactly the same way—is unwise, impractical, and even unfair. But, as we will argue throughout this book, the basic principles of sportsmanship don't vary from one culture to another, from one personality to another. Respect for opponents, for example, might be expressed in a more emotional way by someone from a more emotional culture or by someone with a naturally more expressive personality. But any culture that calls for disrespect toward opponents, or toward other human beings, needs to be challenged. That disrespect for opponents is valued in certain cultures (assuming, for the purposes of argument, that such cultures exist) is no more a defense of disrespectful behavior in athletes than claiming the mass murder of millions of Jews by Nazi Germany was acceptable because the culture of Nazi Germany found it acceptable.

Another prevalent argument is that coaches are paid to coach, not to be a parent, babysitter, or "moral educator." My job is to coach, not teach values. That's a job for families and churches, not coaches. If kids are less respectful nowadays, that's not my fault. I have to work with the hand I've been dealt.

But, you don't have any choice. You're a role model and a moral educator, whether you like it or not. The issue is not whether you, as a coach, choose to convey values; the issue is whether you choose to convey the values of *sportsmanship* and whether you make this teaching a conscious part of your coaching. Would you want your child to play for a coach who wants no part of teaching values? Wouldn't you want your child to be taught to respect others, love the game, and be responsible, trustworthy, and fair?

And of course there's the long-standing objection to sportsmanship—that sports are about winning and losing. Winning is the point—period. That's what we should be teaching our children. Life is competitive. If you want to get ahead, you'd better be realistic about these things. Sports teach you to hate losing, to love winning, and to do whatever is necessary in order to win. If I have to intimidate opponents or officials in order to win, so be it. And if others don't, that's their problem. Sports teach you to make the other guy the loser. On this view, competitiveness is seen as the fundamental virtue—in fact, the only virtue—in sport and in life. When competitiveness in athletes becomes the primary praiseworthy trait, sportsmanship becomes an impediment to athletic virtue.

First of all, in many, if not most, cases it's a mistake to think that teaching and requiring good sportsmanship from your players are inconsistent with the pursuit of victory. In fact, as we'll argue, not taking the pursuit of victory seriously is unsportsmanlike. There have been and continue to be fine coaches who demand both athletic excellence and moral excellence from their players. John Wooden is merely one example of a successful coach who insisted on character and integrity.

But, more important, the view that winning at all costs is what matters is based on a misunderstanding of sport and competition. Competitiveness, properly understood, not only does not conflict with sportsmanship—it requires it. In a 1995 interview for a *60 Minutes* segment on sportsmanship, Kareem Abdul-Jabbar, whose ability to win certainly wasn't stifled by John Wooden's emphasis on sportsmanship, remarked,

UCLA basketball coach John Wooden, winner of 10 NCAA titles.

"Our whole culture here in America has become a lot more vulgar. And I think it's not considered cool to be a good sportsman. You're considered square and soft. . . . There's the whole process of celebration that's gone beyond celebration. It's taunting. I pity the people who are doing this, because they really don't understand: Sport is a step away from the rule of the jungle, and they're trying to move it back towards the jungle, when the strong survive and misuse the weaker in any way that they want. And that's really unfortunate for our whole system of values in our country."

Wrap-Up

As we'll argue in chapter 2, teaching sportsmanship is not a matter of imposing standards of behavior that come from outside the arena of sport. What Kareem reminds us is that unsportsmanlike conduct is the result of misunderstanding the nature of sport. Unsportsmanlike conduct is conduct that is contrary to the nature of sport, and sportsmanlike conduct is conduct that is consistent with the nature of sport. Bad sportsmanship, then, is at least in part the result of bad understanding. To understand why Kareem would say that sport is a step away from the law of the jungle, we'll have to spend some time—pardon the sports metaphor—in the weight room and on the practice field of thinking. We'll have to think about the nature of sport. In this chapter you have begun the process of thinking about these difficult but important issues. But, mostly, we have challenged you with questions that have forced you to reflect on your own experience as a coach. Now we want to help you think not just about your personal experience but also about the nature of the activity you're engaged in.

TWO

Neither are the two arts of music and gymnastic really designed, as is often supposed, the one for the training of the soul, the other for the training of the body.

What then is the real object of them?

I believe, I said, that the teachers of both have in view chiefly the improvement of the soul.

~ Plato, Republic (Jowett translation)

The true athlete should have good character, not be a character.

~ John Wooden

Sportsmanship and the Nature of Sport

In this chapter, we want you to think hard about the very nature of the activity in which you are involved. Perhaps you've never asked yourself, in an explicit way, the most basic question: What is sport? But as we have already suggested, there's little doubt that your approach to coaching probably assumes some answer to this question. In this chapter we'll ask you to make your assumptions explicit—and to examine them. We'll ask you to think explicitly about the nature of sport. At various points, we'll stop and imagine how some coaches might respond to what we're saying. So imagine that you're engaged in a conversation with us. At other times, we'll take a brief time-out to enable you to reflect on the issue that we're raising.

Why Sportsmanship?

Why sportsmanship? Actually, as Kareem's remarks in chapter 1 reminded us, the first question is: Why sport? It's impossible to say why sportsmanship is important—or even what it is—without some understanding of what sport is all about. Why do we play these games? Why do we encourage our children to play them? Why do we include sports in our schools?

Some educators have questioned the value of the competitive experience in an educational setting, on the playing field as well as in the classroom, while others insist that participation in sports is a valuable experience, even a necessary educational experience. Detractors say the competitive situation is debilitating, that it instills bad character traits, that "cooperative learning" ought to displace competitive learning; defenders say that "sport builds character," that competition provides a unique opportunity for learning.

Some of these disagreements run deep, and they ultimately have to do with profoundly different views of what life is all about, but on both sides there's a good deal of confusion about the *nature* of the activity. Why sportsmanship? Why sport? How we answer those questions depends on how we answer another question: What is sport? In other words, what is the *nature* of sport? Of course, this question has generated volumes of learned reflection by anthropologists, sociologists, psychologists, and philosophers. We certainly can't fully address this question here, but it is possible to offer a brief sketch of an answer.

One of the problems we're trying to address is that the American sport culture tends to be antithetical to this kind of theoretical reflection. We assume that we already know what sport is. The only question is how to be good at it. And talking about the nature of sport seems unnecessarily abstract. The truth is, we all operate with some idea about the nature of sport. We're saying that it's something we need to consciously think about.

Thinking about, or not thinking about, the nature of sport has serious consequences. Suppose you think that sport is something we do to escape from the drudgery of work—a kind of pleasant release from the things that really matter. That it's "fun." It's "play." And that its purpose is to help us relax so that we can go back to work, which is what really matters, refreshed. Wouldn't that have an effect on how you would treat your players? Run a practice? Coach a game?

Or say you think that sport is an arena for the strong to triumph over the weak, winners over losers. That it's about winning, and only about winning. Would that view of the nature of sport affect the way you approached coaching? Of course it would. That's why we're asking you to take a step back from the day-to-day pressures of running a practice, preparing for the archrival, dealing with irate parents, and talking to the local radio sportscaster. We're asking you to think about what sort of activity you're involved in, because the ideas and assumptions that you carry into coaching have a profound effect on the young people you coach.

The Nature of Sport

The language we use to talk about sport is revealing. We "play the game," "play ball," "make the play." We call the participants "players." *Sport is a form of play.* Inherent in the idea of play is that, unlike work, we don't have to do it. We freely choose to play. And it's important to note that we *freely* choose to play, not because playing results in something else that is valuable (although it may), but because we enjoy playing. We play because it's fun, exhilarating, beautiful. In philosophical terms, we play because we find the activity of playing *inherently* valuable. That's why historian Johan Huizinga refers to the human species as *homo ludens,* "playing man." Far from being a mere escape from "real life," play is a part of who we are.

Of course, there are other forms of play that aren't sport. Kids horsing around on a jungle gym or simply running around the neighborhood burning up energy is play, but it isn't sport. When parents say to a child, "Go outside and play," they aren't usually thinking about sport. What, then, distinguishes sport from other forms of play? While sport is still play, there is an element of seriousness about it. Although we sometimes use the term "sport" to refer to noncompetitive physical activities such as fishing or horseback riding for pleasure, in the context of school or club athletics, sport takes on this air of seriousness because it involves competition—and because this competition is governed by rules and customs. The rules spell out the nature of the competition, and they establish the boundaries of fairness within which winning is meaningful. But competition does involve winning and losing. Players "play" the game, but they pit their skills and abilities against the skills of opponents, and even against other participants, past, present, and future. Within the context of the game, one player is *better* than another; one team is *better* than another. Because the kind of sport we're concerned with here is competitive, better and worse matter. It's play, but it's serious; it's fun, but it's difficult; it can be exhilarating, but it can be heartbreaking.

Sport, then, is a form of play, a competitive, rule-governed activity that human beings freely choose to engage in. Understanding this, we must play it as if it is absolutely important while never forgetting it's a form of play that, in a certain sense, doesn't really matter. Ultimately, the principles of sportsmanship are based on the delicate balance of playfulness and seriousness that is at the heart of sport.

Time-Out for Reflection

- Which do you emphasize more: the seriousness or the playfulness of competition? If you think in terms of a scale from total playfulness to total seriousness, where do you place yourself on the scale?

- What do you say in practice or during and after a game to remind your players that sport is a form of play? What are some of the common expressions that draw attention to the playful character of sport?

- What do you say to draw attention to the serious side of sport and to its competitive nature? What are some of the common expressions that draw attention to the seriousness of competition?

- Suppose your team has just lost a well-fought game against a superior opponent. How often do you do the following?

  - Say something like "It's only a game" or "Your mother will still love you."

  - Blow up and tell them they didn't want it badly enough.

  - Commend them for their play and their behavior.

  - Commend the opponents for their play and behavior.

  - Punish the team for losing (with an extra practice, extra running, or the like).

Three Perspectives on Competition: Finding the Middle Way

When we forget the balance of playfulness and seriousness, sportsmanship falls by the wayside. Two extreme views of competition are based on a confusion about the balance of playfulness and seriousness in sport. Our intention is to offer a third view, a middle way that preserves this essential balance.

At one extreme is the view that winning is everything and the only thing, that nothing is ever gained in losing except learning that losing is bad. Competition on this model is like war: The opponent is the enemy and the goal is to destroy the enemy. At the other extreme is the view that competition is inherently bad, that all forms of play in which there are winners and losers are unethical, psychologically destructive, educationally ineffective. On this view, only noncompetitive play is acceptable. Sports are acceptable only if they are organized, coached, and taught in such a way that winning—and therefore talent and ability—doesn't matter at all. On this view, "having fun" is the only thing that matters.

The winning-is-everything approach loses track of the spirit of play; the fun-is-everything approach loses track of the seriousness. To the one, we ought to say, "Lighten up," and to the other, "Get serious." From the standpoint of the middle ground on which sport is both playful and serious, both of these extremes are based on the same misunderstanding of the nature of competition.

On one level, competition does involve winners and losers; and, more specifically, if one side wins, the other necessarily loses. But on another level, competition is an opportunity for the development, exercise, and expression of human excellence. Trying to win means trying to do the best I can at the game, trying to be as excellent as possible in all of the ways that the game calls for. But it is precisely my opponent's effort to excel, my opponent's effort to perform better than I do, that gives me the opportunity to strive for excellence. By the same token, I make it possible for my opponent to strive for excellence. In that sense I ought to be thankful for a great opponent. On one level opponents "oppose" each other; on another level they are engaged in what Drew Hyland calls a "mutual striving for excellence." In a 1978 essay called "Competition and Friendship," Hyland points out that the word "competition" derives from the Latin *competitio,* meaning "to question or strive together." If it's valuable to play, then my opponent is valuable to me; without an opponent I can't play. On the playing field, "cooperative" and "competitive" learning are not opposites, for good competition is cooperation.

Of course, it's little wonder that some people would conclude that competition is inherently bad if their competitive experiences have been characterized by the winning-is-everything attitude. If winning is everything and you're better than I am, then what's the point? If I'm going to lose, it's pretty obvious that my only rational choice is to refuse to compete. Or, if I am better than you and you will get nothing from losing to me, then my beating you is nothing short of exploitation. Both of those situations would be morally repugnant.

At the other extreme, if you teach kids that winning doesn't matter at all, you're not being honest about the nature of competition. If it doesn't matter at all whether I win or lose, if it doesn't matter at all whether I throw the ball well or poorly, what's the point? If the winning-is-everything extreme is morally repugnant, the winning-is-nothing extreme is morally inane. A beginning youth league might well employ a rule that all players play a certain number of minutes to allow all of the participants an opportunity to learn the skills of the game, but employing such a rule to downplay the competitive aspect of the game misses the point of competition.

To steer a course between these extremes, we have to articulate the value of participating in the game and the opportunity that *participation* affords. At the risk of combating clichés with clichés, we do need to return to the notion that, at some deeper level, it's not whether you win or lose—after all, somebody must lose for somebody else to win—but how you play the game. In fact, we can take this idea one step further: It's not just how *you* play the game that ultimately matters, but how the *game* is played, for it is participation in that game that is valuable. How I play the game contributes to the quality of that game for me, my teammates, my coach, and my opponents—even spectators and the community.

It's not whether you win or lose, but what kind of game everyone gets to participate in. Central to the game is the effort of the participants to win, and without the participants' commitment to winning, there is no game. It is not, however, the winning itself that ultimately matters, but the sorts of things we experience and come to understand by playing the game and the opportunities for human excellence that playing the game affords. This perspective is likely to be met with skepticism in some quarters. If you tell your players that winning isn't everything, will they try as hard to win? Will it matter enough to them?

Don't misunderstand what we're saying. We believe that winning really matters—and that it should matter. But it matters within the context of participating in an exhilarating experience of trying to become excellent and learning things about ourselves. The main problem with the winning-is-everything attitude is that it diminishes the importance of all the other good things about sport. It's like going to a good movie and saying the only good thing about it was how it turned out. An understanding of the richness of sport helps us sustain the balance of playfulness and seriousness, and this very balance provides space for other important values—including sportsmanship—to flourish. In fact, what we're saying is that competitiveness—striving to win—is an essential part of sportsmanship.

Sport and Virtue

One of the assumptions we make in this book is that coaches—and, for that matter, administrators, parents, fans, officials, and everyone else involved in youth athletics—are moral educators, whether they want to be or not. That does not mean that they are moral indoctrinators—indeed, they should not indoctrinate. It does mean, however, that, inescapably, they play a role in the formation of character.

For this reason, it is important to understand that sportsmanship is not just a matter of acceptable behavior but of *excellence of character*—or, in the language of the classical tradition, *sportsmanship is a virtue*. It is not altogether coincidental that there has been a return to the classical understanding of virtue, to "virtue-centered ethics," right at a time when so many of our athletic superstars in professional and big-time college sports have become models of anything and everything but good character. It is particularly sad because sport has long provided an arena in which the central ethical concept has been excellence of character. Part of the purpose of this book is to reclaim the moral language that was—and to a large extent still is—part of the great athletic traditions harkening all the way back to the Olympian ideals that we continue to celebrate every four years as well as the language of classical ethical thought that harkens all the way back to ancient Greek philosophy.

There are some pitfalls to this language. The English word "virtue," in certain contexts, has the connotation of moral purity, of having avoided the stain of vice. In that context, one is virtuous by not doing something. We mean by *virtue* not moral purity but excellence of character. Both "virtue" and "excellence" have been used as translations of the classical Greek *aretē*, the central concept in Plato's and Aristotle's ethical thought, and it is that concept of virtue that we have in mind.

When we speak of a return to a virtue-centered ethics, we have in mind the turn from ethics centered on principles and rules for right action and good conduct to ethics centered on the importance of good character. Sportsmanship, then, is not just about following rules, behaving a certain way because that's the way you're supposed to behave; it's about what sort of human beings we choose to become. When William Bennett, former Secretary of Education, published *The Book of Virtues* in 1993, a good part of what he had in mind was the classical notion of virtue as *excellence of character*. His notion is that stories can provide models of excellent character. Our notion—and, of course, it's not our notion, but a very old one—is that athletic competition can provide an arena for the *practice* of virtue—that is, for development of excellent character.

Because virtue is at least in part a matter of deeply ingrained habits, it makes sense to say that a person can practice virtue. The English word "ethics" derives from the Greek word for habit, *ethos*. If I lack self-discipline, I need opportunities—not overwhelmingly difficult ones to begin with—to develop the habit of self-discipline. If I lack courage and self-confidence, I need the opportunity to develop courage and self-confidence. Likewise, if sportsmanship is a virtue, it makes sense to say that one can practice sportsmanship. It is essential to recognize that all the principles or rules for behavior that we'll articulate in the following chapters are grounded in the notion that they develop excellence of character.

There may be a good deal of disagreement about exactly how to flesh out the content of an excellent character. It would be impossible here to attempt to list and think through even the most historically important recommendations concerning the central human virtues: wisdom, courage, self-control, justice, honesty, autonomy, humility, benevolence, love, authenticity, compassion, responsibility, respectfulness . . . the list would be quite long. What is clear, though, is that sport requires and shapes character traits. It's not by any means the only arena—so are the classroom, the music practice room, and, in most households, the room with the biggest TV set—but it's an important one. How you set up a practice, talk about the game, respond to discipline problems—everything you do—sets the tone, takes a stand on what sort of character traits you value. How you respond to a lazy player who merely goes through the motions of a strenuous drill, a player's taunting of an opponent, a player of mediocre talent whose effort was superb—all of these responses tell young athletes what kind of character you value, what sort of human beings they should aspire to be. In short, we're better off to admit that we are moral educators, try to think as clearly about these difficult issues as we can, and develop our athletic programs accordingly. Coaches don't simply stamp out human character like, say, automobiles in a factory. In fact, one of the things we have to remember is that coaches have to make good judgments not only about the abilities and limits of athletic ability but also about the natural dispositions and limitations of character. But coaches do provide an opportunity for the practice of virtue.

In fleshing out the virtue of sportsmanship, you'll come to see that practicing sportsmanship means practicing an attitude of respect. Respect is an attitude of positive evaluation, a recognition of something, some reality that merits understanding and attentiveness. To respect something is to value it and treat it as worthy in its own right. To respect something, I have to overcome my inclination to be selfish, my inclination to see the thing only in terms of my own needs and interests. To respect my parents or to respect my country, for example, is to esteem or to honor something outside myself and to realize that there are right and wrong ways to act in relation to these independent realities.

To be a good sport, I must understand my situation and see things broadly, not simply in terms of self-centered desires to win, to be famous, or to be mentioned in the headlines of the local newspaper. As a player or participant, I should respect opponents, teammates, officials, the coach, and, in the broadest sense, the very activity in which I am engaged. It is important to remember, however, that we are talking not simply about rules for behavior but about the *habit of respect*—a habit of respect that becomes a part of someone's character.

Time-Out for Reflection

- How often do the following words or expressions come out of your mouth?

  - Integrity
  - Class, class act
  - Dignity
  - Respect
  - Sportsmanship
  - Honor
  - Humility

- The list of cardinal virtues for classical Greek civilization included wisdom, self-control, courage, and justice. What kinds of situations call for these cardinal virtues?

- Come up with your own list of virtues. If you believe that sport builds character, what are the character traits, the virtues, that you think sport builds?

- Put into your own words what it means to have an attitude of respect. Do you think that young people today are less inclined to exhibit this attitude? If so, why has this come about?

Sport, Good Judgment, and Self-Understanding

As a moral educator, you have to make good judgments yourself, but it bears mentioning that you are also providing the arena in which your players can develop good judgment. We may be able to say in a general way what sportsmanship is—and you may be able to explain it to your players—but that doesn't mean we can tell you exactly what the sportsmanlike thing to do will be in every particular situation. And you will not be able to tell your players in every situation how to apply these principles. The practice and development of good character, as well as its exercise, require good judgment. As we articulate the principles of good sportsmanship in the chapters that follow, the first thing that will come to mind for anyone with athletic experience is that it's often difficult to determine in a particular situation what is the appropriate way to exercise respect for opponents (chapter 3), respect for teammates (chapter 4), respect for officials (chapter 5), respect for the game (chapter 6), or respect between players and coaches (chapter 7).

If an opponent repeatedly demonstrates disrespect for me and for the game, for example, how do I respond in such a way as to demonstrate that I understand my need for a good opponent and my respect for the game? We will provide examples of difficult situations, and we encourage you to think them through, discuss them, and try to figure out how to respond in light of the principles of sportsmanship that we articulate here. We hasten to point out that the difficulty that some situations present for the realization of these principles doesn't mean that the principles are invalid. Many situations and many actions and responses by athletes are clear as day, and we'll provide examples of that nature as well. In that sense, good stories about heroes and villains are essential. Indeed, the fact that decisions in light of principles are sometimes difficult doesn't mean that we should abandon principles. It is precisely when the situations are difficult that we need to stress deliberation in light of principles.

One of the dangers of a simplistic approach to the idea that sport builds character is that we can forget the essential role of deliberation and judgment and understanding, especially of self-understanding. Sport handled well provides an opportunity to understand the importance of truthfulness about oneself and about one's relationships to others. Self-understanding has largely to do with coming to terms with limits—understanding what I *can* do and what I *can't* do. Ultimately, all true possibility comes from understanding limits, for knowing the limits of what I am capable of means knowing what I am capable of. In an athletic contest, that kind of understanding is essential from both the technical standpoint of trying to figure out how to beat an opponent and the moral standpoint of trying to figure out what sort of person I am capable of being. I have to know my own strengths and weaknesses to compete well. If I'm a gymnast like Shawn Johnson, I want to develop a floor exercise routine that takes advantage of my daring athleticism; if I'm more like Nastia Liukin, I want to emphasize balletic grace.

If I'm a baseball player with no power but good speed, I need to develop my skills as a slap hitter and I'd better be able to lay down a good bunt. If I'm an archer with a tendency to get complacent after shooting three or four good ends, I need to admit that I have this weakness. I might need to develop the habit of telling myself that no matter how good the last end was, I could shoot a few points higher if I would only bear down harder.

Of course, self-understanding of limits includes the recognition of *apparent* limits, which can lead to one of the most rewarding athletic experiences—overcoming apparent limits. Sometimes young athletes (and old ones) think they are capable of much more than they are, and sometimes they are capable of more—sometimes much more—than they think they are. Knowing which is which is not easy, but it's central to the athletic experience. To bombard young athletes with the fiction that anything is possible if they work hard enough, want it bad enough, or visualize it long enough may sometimes be effective locker-room rhetoric, but the truth can be effective, too. Why not say to a young athlete, when the occasion calls for it, "I'm not going to tell you that anything is possible, because it isn't; but I do think you are capable of much more than you realize"?

U.S. gymnasts Shawn Johnson and Nastia Liukin.

Of course, if winning is everything, then there is no room for self-understanding about limits. If winning is everything, then anything is possible. If we lost the game, then we should have done something else to win. But there's a difference between reasonably exhorting young athletes to do more than they think they are capable of and pushing them to cheat, to use steroids, or to psychologically self-destruct. There's a difference, for example, between demanding fitness of a young female gymnast within the limits of her growing body and driving her to anorexic eating habits that will carry over into the rest of her life.

Sportsmanship requires an understanding that all of us are finite human beings with finite strengths, that we are all limited; but at the same time, it requires that we understand how athletic competition gives us an opportunity to *excel,* to develop ourselves and in a certain sense to transcend ourselves, to become better. The word "sportsmanship" is shorthand for a whole complex of character traits that athletic competition should instill in our young people, but inextricably bound up with the development of that character is the judgment and the understanding—*seeing the way things are*—that make it possible to exercise that character.

And, perhaps even more important, because athletic competition always involves understanding ourselves in relation to others, it provides an arena for the development of judgment about human relations. I must not only know my own strengths and weaknesses but also my strengths and weaknesses in relation to my opponents' and to my teammates' strengths and weaknesses. I have to pit my abilities against an opponent in such a way as to gain a relative advantage—and usually that doesn't mean I get the opportunity simply to pit my strength against my opponent's weakness. My crosscourt forehand may be my strongest shot, but my opponent's may be stronger; even though I'd rather hit my forehand, I may realize that backhand rallies will give me the edge. And, as I seek the advantage that might allow me to win, I have to keep sight of the deeper level at which our competition binds us together. I can come to understand and respect the efforts of others, and I can come to respect and admire the achievements and talents of others. In a team sport, I have to fit my abilities into the web of interrelations that makes up a team. If, for example, I shoot a basketball like I was born with boxing gloves on, I need to set picks for my teammates who can shoot. I have to understand the mystery of the whole becoming greater than the sum of the parts—that, when the team clicks, the individual participants get back more than they put into it.

Time-Out for Reflection

- Apply these reflections about limits and apparent limits to yourself. What are the weaknesses that you need to be aware of? Strengths? Think not just in terms of your technical prowess as a coach but in terms of moral character.

- There's a saying that "Your greatest strength is your greatest weakness." What does that mean?

- What do you do and say to your players to help them understand their own limits, their own strengths and weaknesses as athletes and as human beings?

- What do you do and say to your players to help them overcome apparent limits?

- Rate yourself on a scale from an overwillingness to accept limits at one extreme to the belief that there are no limits at the other. Remember that we're talking here not about locker-room rhetoric but about understanding the way things are.

- One of the taglines in Nike's ad campaign during the Atlanta Olympic Games was "You don't win silver, you lose gold." What are the implications of that sentiment?

Sport, Humility, and Wisdom

Athletic achievement is a matter of hard work, determination, and practice, but it's also a matter of talent and circumstance, of streaks and inexplicable chemistry and magic moments. Even in a culture that often encourages unabashed self-congratulation and self-adulation, many of our greatest athletes react to their achievements with gestures and remarks of thankfulness, humility, even a kind of reverence: Björn Borg falling to his knees at Wimbledon, Roger Maris so humbled by hitting his 61st home run that his teammates had to physically shove him back out of the dugout so the fans could cheer him. Some athletes express this experience in religious terms, "thanking God for the opportunity." Whether we understand this experience in religious terms or not, in part we do experience—and we should experience—great talent, a great game or series, a great hitting or shooting streak, the chemistry of a great team, as a "gift," an opportunity that is "given" to us.

Great talents can be squandered or developed, but, in the end, talent is something a person is lucky enough to have, not something that he or she earns (and, as the behavior of some of the most talented individuals all too clearly reveals, we shouldn't infer from the presence of talent that its possessor deserves to possess it). Almost paradoxically, the experience of great talent, if we think about it honestly, is an occasion for humility and thankfulness. Michael Jordan may have worked very hard at what he did so well, but so have thousands of other basketball players—and there has been only one Michael Jordan. His talent was a thing of beauty: It's something for us to admire and for him to be proud of, but at the same time it's something for him—and for us—to be thankful for. Without the countless hours of grueling training, Michael Phelps would not have won a single Olympic gold medal, but without the unique physical attributes that his particular genetic mix blessed him with—right down to the unusual proportions of his body—all of the training in the world would not have produced 14 career Olympic gold medals, the most of any athlete ever.

One of the consequences of understanding talent as a gift is the recognition that talent carries with it special responsibilities. In the movie *Hoosiers,* when the new basketball coach tells the most talented young athlete in town that he has a gift, he is at the same time exhorting him to develop it, to come to deserve it, to let it contribute. As a rule, the greater the talent, the greater the responsibility. Although sport provides one of the few arenas in which we can openly talk about natural ability, it's worth noting here that this rule is not restricted to the playing field.

Along the same lines, great athletic events and achievements are often experienced as opportunities for which the participants and spectators feel grateful. Ask a great hitter in the middle of a streak (or, maybe better, after it's over) how he experiences his accomplishment. Years of practice and effort are the prerequisites for a streak, and yet, like a slump, there is a sense in which *it just happens.* And there is a sense in which it can't be forced. Good coaches know the expression "Let it happen," and they know the right moments to use it. In *Zen in the Art of Archery,* German philosopher Eugen Herrigel recounts the six years he spent studying archery with a Zen master in Japan. The discipline and dedication and effort are monumental, but the master tells him that the goal of all this hard work is to get to the point at which "it" will shoot the arrows, not him. The Taoists call this *wu-wei,* letting things happen spontaneously and naturally. After winning the men's individual gold medal in archery in the 1996 Summer Olympics in Atlanta, Justin Huish, a 21-year-old Californian, remarked, "I was in a fog, just trying to see gold in my sight and let it rip."

In *Life on the Run,* Bill Bradley describes his love of basketball this way:

> The money and the championships are reasons I play, but what I'm addicted to are the nights like tonight when something special happens on the court. The experience is one of beautiful isolation. It cannot be deduced from the self-evident, like a philosophical proposition. It cannot be generally agreed upon, like an empirically verifiable fact, and it is far more than a passing emotion. It is as if a lightning bolt strikes, brings insight into an uncharted area of human experience. (pp. 220-221)

In *A River Runs Through It,* Norman Maclean describes the art of casting a fly rod in terms of this same mysterious combination of determined hard work and the humility to let it happen:

> *My father was very sure about certain matters pertaining to the universe. To him, all good things—trout as well as eternal salvation—come by grace and grace comes from art and art does not come easy. (p. 4)*

No work, no grace. But, by the same token, work alone cannot achieve it; it cannot be forced. Maclean puts it this way:

> *Well, until man is redeemed he will always take a fly rod too far back, just as natural man always overswings with an ax or golf club and loses all his power somewhere in the air; only with a rod it's worse, because the fly often comes so far back it gets caught behind in a bush or rock. (p. 3)*

The son of a Presbyterian minister, Maclean chooses to call it "grace"; the Zen master says "it" shoots the arrow, that the release of the arrow is like the snow falling from the end of a bamboo leaf. In American sports lingo, we talk about athletes being "in the zone," "on fire," "shooting lights out," "unconscious." It's that experience of being present when something wonderful happens. We come to appreciate just how much the great moments in sport are a gift for which we should be grateful, because we've all been in the situation of saying, "It just didn't happen for me today," "I just didn't have it today," or "I tried my best, but it wasn't in the cards." When it does happen for us, it's wise to feel proud of our achievement but at the same time lucky to be there.

In that sense, the athletic experience goes beyond the development of character and the calculative understanding of one's strengths and weaknesses; it is an opportunity for a kind of wisdom. Although we may not go so far as to endorse the total selflessness of Zen Buddhism, we can say that sport sometimes does provide an experience of a kind of spirituality that transcends the arrogant egoism that characterizes so much of our culture. The experience in sport of great moments and great talent, far from encouraging the arrogant egoism that we see too often on our TVs, is an occasion for a kind of selfless humility. And that experience of selfless humility can be mysteriously enriching.

We can agree with the Zen master that this is the same spirituality that humans have sought in all the activities that can be done either well or poorly, all of the activities that require dedication, hard work, and grace. In giving yourself over to the activity, something happens to you. Great musicians, like great athletes, give themselves over to the music, and the music comes over them. The same could be said of great writers, dancers, cooks, carpenters, and a host of others. By giving themselves over to something, by giving themselves up to the activity, they are enlarged by it.

A Coach's Guidelines for Teaching Sportsmanship

Throughout the book we will punctuate our discussions of the principles of sportsmanship with questions and suggestions about how you might go about teaching and promoting these principles in your coaching. Each chapter in part II will include "An Example of Teaching Sportsmanship" with specific suggestions for a particular sport. In the end, the application of these principles to your day-to-day coaching is something you will have to do for yourself. The application of principles requires good judgment, and you're the one who has to develop and exercise that judgment. Nonetheless, we thought it might be helpful to provide some suggestions for how you might go about putting these principles into practice.

The main purpose of this book is to offer something that is largely missing from our contemporary sport culture: an articulation of the principles of sportsmanship that is grounded in an understanding of the nature of sport. Here, based on our experience as coaches, athletes, and fans—as "students of the game" with regard to at least a few sports—we will throw out some ideas for how an understanding of these principles might show up in the practice of coaching. In chapter 7, we will argue that one of the coach's obligations toward the players is to exhibit and teach them the principles of sportsmanship. As we see it, there are three approaches to the teaching of sportsmanship: teaching by explicit instruction, teaching by example, and practicing sportsmanship. Deciding how much you depend on explicit instruction and how much you depend on having your players practice sportsmanship is a function of the age of the players (the older they are, the more you can explicitly explain to them) and your own abilities and personality.

Regardless of your personality, as you try to get players to form the habit of sportsmanship, you'll have to depend on a variety of approaches. The most obvious device is the use of rules and punishments for the violation of rules. But remember that respect for others, the cornerstone of sportsmanlike behavior, requires first and foremost the perspective to see things from the other's point of view. And many of the activities that promote the habit and perspective of sportsmanship—say, the postgame handshake—are not activities required by rules but by custom and tradition. They take on the character of meaningful rituals that become as much a part of the sport as the rules. Remember that you can develop, even invent, rituals that can become a part of the sport—or at least a part of your team's identity.

Here, then, are some general guidelines for teaching sportsmanship to young athletes. These guidelines would apply to any sport that you might coach within a scholastic setting.

Be a good role model.   As a coach, you must constantly keep in mind that your actions do, in fact, speak louder than your words. No matter what you say, what you do will have an effect on your players. You must do everything you can to show your players what it means to be a good sport by treating opposing players and coaches, officials, team members, and the sport in which you participate with respect. An obvious corollary: Admit to your players when you fall short of your own sportsmanship ideals.

Emphasize sportsmanship from the beginning.   The process of teaching sportsmanship should start early, from your first contact with players. If you're recruiting a player to come out for the team or a player comes to you to discuss trying out, what you say will set the tone for your relationship with that player. At the first team meeting with your players, you should explain how much you value sportsmanship. Tell them what your expectations are, how you understand the basic principles of sportsmanship, and why these principles are important.

Talk about combining seriousness and playfulness.   Since the principles of sportsmanship are based on the very nature of sport, and sport is a form of competitive play, explain to your players that sport is "serious fun." Help them understand that bad sportsmanship is often a matter of being "too serious," of forgetting that there's more to sport than winning, and in some cases, a matter of not being serious enough, of forgetting that striving to be excellent and striving to win within the rules and customs of the game are essential parts of competition. Try to show this balance in your own attitude and in your comments. Be serious when it's called for; cut up, kid around, and have fun when it's called for. How you express this balance will in part depend on your own personality, but the need for a balance between playfulness and seriousness is not a matter of personal preference or personality. It comes from the nature of the activity you're engaging in, competitive play. Take your responsibilities seriously, but don't take yourself too seriously.

Talk about the relationship between sportsmanship and success.   Make sure your players understand that "success" in sport is not merely a matter of achieving victory and that victory without sportsmanship, dignity, and honor is hollow. At the same time, try to show your players that respect for the team and your sport, as well as respect between the players and the coach, might help develop habits and talents that will improve your chances of winning.

Regularly use the language of sportsmanship.   The language of sportsmanship should become a regular part of your coaching vocabulary. Don't leave this language behind after the first team meeting. The language of "respect" should be heard by your players often. If you earn their respect, the language you use around them will become a part of their way of looking at things. Never underestimate the power of language. The right words make it possible to understand things we couldn't otherwise understand.

Expect sportsmanship in practice as well as in games.   Since we are encouraging you to develop the habits of good sportsmanship in your players, don't reserve instruction for games only. Expect good behavior—the habit of showing respect—in practice.

Establish team rules, customs, rituals, and traditions that reinforce the principles of sportsmanship.   While it is crucial to talk about the basic principles of sportsmanship, it is probably even more important to be specific about your expectations.

Establish specific team rules that promote good sportsmanship. It's a good idea to list the rules and place them in the context of the principles of sportsmanship. If you demand 100 percent effort at all times, then explain this demand with reference to respecting your opponents, your teammates, and the game. As much as possible, be specific about how you expect your players to relate to opponents, officials, and each other. When the opportunity arises, try to develop customs, rituals, and traditions that will promote sportsmanship. Some customs and rituals you can simply demand, like the postgame handshake. Others develop out of the special relations and situations; some of them the players develop on their own. Take advantage of those developments.

Encourage players to take the perspective of other participants. Since sportsmanship demands proper *perspective,* help players to understand and imaginatively to appreciate others' points of view. This is analogous to the moral education of a child, when a parent sometimes says something like, "How would it make you feel if someone did that to you?" Talk about how opponents and officials might look at you and your players.

Develop clear guidelines for dealing with unsportsmanlike behavior. Make it clear to your players from the beginning of the season how you will deal with actions that violate the principles of sportsmanship. If you decide not to allow taunting, showboating, or arguing with officials, tell the players what the specific penalty (or gradations of penalties) will be if the rules are violated. You can spell out the sequence of possible punishments and explain that you will decide how serious the violation has been—in other words, you don't have to decide in advance what the penalty for every possible violation will be, but you do have to be clear that there are consequences for violations. Be clear about the process. If you'll make the decisions, say that. If you'll allow the team to be involved, say that.

Reinforce good sportsmanship. If good sportsmanship matters to you, show the players, parents, and fans that it matters by rewarding good behavior in some manner. The most obvious way to do this is through praise, respectful behavior, and playing time. At the end of the season, make sure that team awards include sportsmanship, either as a separate award or as a necessary condition for all awards.

Communicate the importance of sportsmanship to parents. Before the season starts, meet with parents and explain to them the value you place on sportsmanship. Enlist their help and support in reinforcing your expectations with their children.

Communicate the importance of sportsmanship to fans. Depending on the situation in which you coach, some kind of public announcement concerning sportsmanship is important. You might address this issue over the public-address system at a game or in a printed handout. You can encourage your school or league officials to adopt rules concerning the misbehavior of fans at home games or matches. Try to develop an educational campaign at your school or in your league or organization promoting the ideals of sportsmanship among fans. Rituals at the beginning of a game showing respect for the opponents can help set the tone for the fans. Your remarks at social functions, postgame interviews on the radio, and so on can also set the tone.

Talk about news stories concerning sportsmanship with your players. Since most of your players are probably sports fans, use current sporting events as an opportunity for discussing sportsmanship with them. When a famous athlete does something controversial or especially laudable, ask your players what they think about the event. Ask them what they would do if they were the coach. Discuss with them how you would deal with that sort of behavior. To some extent, you can help them to see which famous athletes deserve our respect and which do not.

Talk about specific incidents with your players. Encourage your players to bring up incidents that happen to them in sports. Take advantage of things that come up to discuss sportsmanship with your players.

Promote reflectiveness by asking questions. Remember that you are a teacher and that good teaching often involves asking the right questions rather than giving the students carefully packaged answers. Encourage players to think for themselves and make their own reasoned judgments about their experiences or examples you call attention to.

Talk about the history of your sport with players. Talk with your athletes about the historical traditions, innovations, and heroes of your sport in order to broaden their perspective and enrich their sense of participating in something bigger than themselves. Tell good stories. Encourage players to read about the history of their sport in order to develop a respect for the fullness of the game.

Expect players to know the rule book. To encourage players to respect the game as well as the officials, encourage them to study the rule book. Ask them questions about their interpretation of difficult situations if they were officiating. Play "You make the call."

Show by your actions and your words that you care, that what you're trying to teach is important. No matter how much your players may seem to resist you, many of your values will become theirs. Let them know that it matters how they behave, what kind of human beings they will be, whether they do things well or poorly.

Don't forget to have fun. Remember, it's a game. It's serious, it matters, but it's play. Show your players that what they're doing matters, but don't take yourself too seriously. If no one is having fun, you're not playing a game anymore.

Wrap-Up

Why sportsmanship? Because the nature of sport requires it. Sport understood as rule-governed competitive athletic play requires—and therefore can teach—certain character traits. Without sportsmanship, sport is no longer sport; the game is no longer a game. If the game is valuable—if we play the game for its joy, for its educational value, for its intrinsic beauty, for the truth about ourselves that it opens up—then sportsmanship is indispensable.

Why sportsmanship? Because it matters what sort of human beings we are—and what sort of human beings our children become. Because it's better for human beings to be courageous, disciplined, fair, honest, responsible, humble, and wise than not to be. The complex of character traits that we refer to as the virtue of sportsmanship is "useful"—good character helps us to win games, run a business, develop friendships—but we should be careful not to reduce sportsmanship to a mere expediency. Why sportsmanship? Because good character is good for its own sake, whether we are "rewarded" for it or not. Or, in traditional ethical terms, sportsmanship is its own reward.

PART II

The Principles of Sportsmanship

THREE

It was a long shot. They measured it at 565. Anyway, I used to have a terrible habit . . . the funny thing about the home run is . . . that I had a terrible habit of running around the bases with my head down, you know, because I didn't want to embarrass the pitcher. I know he was embarrassed enough already, especially one that long. As I come around second, I'm getting ready to get to third base, with my head down, I hear Frank Crossetti, the third base coach, holler, "Hey, look out!" And I looked up . . . and Billy Martin was on third when I hit the ball . . . he was tagged up like it was a long fly, and I almost ran into him. Of course, he's running on into the plate laughing, and I'm right behind him.

~ Mickey Mantle

If I were to choose one word to describe the Helsinki Games, that word would be "graciousness." The graciousness and kindness of the Finns toward all visitors. The graciousness of the competitors for each other; of the victors toward the vanquished; of the vanquished toward the victors.

~ Brutus Hamilton, U.S. track and field coach, 1952 Olympic Games

Respect for Opponents

OPPONEI

LEARN CAPABILITY UNDERSTANDING

In the 1987 movie *Wall Street*, Gordon Gekko, a Wall Street financial broker only thinly fictionalized, tells his young protégé that he's not in it for the money but because he really enjoys crushing people. Without vigilantly cultivated principles of decency and fairness, the competitive culture of Wall Street can be sadistically ruthless. But lest we blame it all on culture, consider the cruelty that young children sometimes inflict on each other. The truth is, it's a rare saint among us who has never felt the urge to crush an enemy or a rival—or, for that matter, a friend, a lover, or a close family member.

That is not to say we are all one step away from *Lord of the Flies* savagery—for it's just as easy to point to remarkable acts of unselfish sacrifice or charitable forgiveness instead of retaliation. But we humans are indeed capable—whether by enculturation, nature, or original sin—of ruthless dehumanization of our fellow human beings. Add to that state of affairs a competitive situation such as sport, populate it with adolescents (not to mention a few adults who are trying to relive their adolescence), and things can quickly get out of hand.

Respect for opponents is not something that young athletes will naturally develop. It will be obvious to the coach who takes the principles of sportsmanship seriously that this is a problem area. Since the central focus of every practice session and every game is to beat the opponent, it's easy to turn opponents into enemies. And, to make matters worse, since many of the opponents they face will treat them with nothing but disrespect, the natural tendency will be to respond in kind.

Many of the principles of sportsmanship we'll articulate in the following chapters are directly related to the purpose of winning, and for that reason they will be more obvious to the athletes. In a team sport, young athletes can easily see that they need their teammates to win. That may not automatically result in respect for them, but it certainly lays the foundation for it. Likewise, it's not hard for them to understand that a good coach is essential for winning. But, at least on the surface, the situation is different with opponents. An opponent is not someone I need, but someone I'm trying to beat—someone who's trying to foil my every effort. In order to win, I don't have to respect an opponent. Far from it. In fact, some coaches are convinced that you can't beat an opponent you have respect for. Kids nowadays, the argument goes, have to pump themselves up in order to perform—and not just in football and hockey. The top tennis players today routinely pump their fists after winning a point. Even sprinters. When someone asked a top American sprinter about his screaming and chest thumping, he responded, "This is war." That attitude is certainly widespread.

But isn't there a difference between trying to kill an enemy in war and trying to outrun an opponent in a footrace? Is it really necessary to pretend that we're at war in order to get motivated to give our best in sports? By all accounts, Jesse Owens did not need to pump himself up into a warlike fit of rage to win four gold medals at the 1936 Berlin Olympics, even though, indeed, we were on the eve of an actual war with Germany. Chris Evert didn't have to shake her fist at her opponent after winning a point to be one of the most fiercely competitive athletes in the history of tennis. If it's true that kids nowadays do have to work themselves into a violent frenzy in order to be competitive—and the truth is, plenty of kids nowadays don't—then the response is not that we have to coach or educate them differently because they are different from the kids of previous generations; rather, if they are different it's because we've coached and educated them differently, and because all of the cultural forces have educated them differently. In education there's always this chicken-and-egg situation.

In other words, today's kids aren't different: Just like the kids of every generation, *they can learn*. They can learn to think that taunting an opponent with total disrespect is "part of the game"—or they can learn why respect for an opponent is a fundamental part of competition. And, although many situations will present great difficulties for applying the principle, we can help them develop the good judgment that difficult situations require. That they can learn, of course, means that we, their parents, teachers, and coaches, can teach them. Rather than throwing up our hands and saying they're different, we can get our hands dirty and try to teach them why respect for an opponent makes sense.

Why Respect Opponents?

Why should I respect my opponent? On the surface, it's not obvious. It requires that we think about the nature of competition. It's only at a deeper level of understanding that we come to see that we should respect an opponent. Given that understanding, we can then cultivate the *habit* of respecting an opponent, and we can develop customs and rules that promote that respect; but understanding the reason for it requires that we think.

Opponents Provide Opportunities to Excel

Although it isn't at first obvious, if we do step back from the heat of battle and think about the nature of competition, the principle of respect for opponents is remarkably simple. If participation in athletic competition is valuable, then a good opponent makes it possible for me to do something valuable—no opponent, no game. In chapter 2 we argued that competition, reflectively understood, provides us with an opportunity to excel both as athletes and as human beings. Opponents who do their best to beat me "oppose" my best effort to beat them, and on that level my opponent's best effort can be downright infuriating; however, if I step back and think about what's going on, I realize that my opponent's effort to beat me has given me an opportunity, has challenged me to do my best.

Just after she announced her retirement, Chris Evert was asked to name the best match she had ever played. Initially, she referred to all of the Grand Slam finals she played against Martina Navratilova. Five of those, a good tennis fan will remember, she lost to Martina at Wimbledon. Pushed to pick one match, she finally named one of the Wimbledon matches she lost as the best match she ever played. Martina brought out the best in her. It's arguable, along the same lines, that John McEnroe lost his heart for tennis when his great rival, Björn Borg, retired. Muhammad Ali needed his Joe Frazier. Great athletes need great opponents to excel. All athletes need opponents, or they couldn't play the game; all athletes need good opponents who challenge them to excel—that is, well-matched opponents who give their best. For that reason, respect for the opponent goes to the very heart of sportsmanship.

Human Excellence Is Worthy of Respect

A second point needs to be made here. Far from taking away from my efforts to excel, the excellence of a fairly matched opponent contributes to my efforts; but, in addition, human excellence—whether of skill or of moral fiber—is in itself worthy of respect. If I think it's worthwhile to try to achieve excellence, then I should respect excellence in others. Even as we compete for the title, how can I not appreciate in others the achievements, the skill, or the character I so desire to see in myself? A beautiful backhand is a beautiful backhand, whether it's mine or yours; a perfect set in volleyball is a perfect set; a great effort is a great effort. Sport, then, is an arena for learning to gracefully acknowledge and to respect excellence in others. Respect for an opponent, then, also has to do with the respect for human excellence that our very decision to play the game seriously commits us to.

Time-Out for Reflection

- Come up with three stories from your experiences as a player or coach that exhibit in a striking fashion the principle of respect for an opponent—stories you might want to tell your players to give them models. Come up with three stories from your actual experience as a player or coach that exhibit in a striking fashion disrespect for an opponent.

- Are there other situations in life in which it is difficult but important to respect a person with whom you're competing? What are other situations a young person might confront in which it might be easier to see that respecting an opponent is more appropriate than, for example, hating one?

- Compare the attitude of respect with other attitudes you might take toward opponents. For example, explain the difference between respecting an opponent and liking an opponent.

- Are there ever situations in sport in which it is appropriate to fail to respect an opponent? If there are, what actions are appropriate to show this disrespect? For example, at the end of the game, should we always, without exception, attempt to shake the hands of our opponents? Should a coach teach players that this requirement is absolute?

In most sports, how well you do requires that you respond to what your opponent does—or that you make the opponent respond to what you're doing. If your opponent has an excellent backhand, you'd better take note of it. But respecting your opponent's excellent backhand doesn't mean that you'll put less effort into trying to win. It means that you aspire to hit a backhand well, too.

Showing Respect for Opponents

Once you think about the nature of competition, the general principle of respect for opponents makes sense. But what does all of this mean in practical terms?

Martina Navratilova and Chris Evert, each the winner of 18 Grand Slam singles titles.

Giving Your Best Effort

First, let's talk about what respect for opponents doesn't mean. It doesn't mean being "nice" to the opponent, although it does mean being civil. It most assuredly doesn't mean that you don't try to beat your opponent—that you don't take winning seriously. Anything less than your best effort to win is just as disrespectful as trying to win by cheating or by disrupting your opponent's mental state in ways that have nothing to do with the sport. Competition is only a "mutual striving for excellence" if both sides strive to win. I should give my best effort, and my opponents owe their best efforts to me. In fact, my respect for opponents should include demanding their best efforts to beat me. If a championship (or, in the pros, a lot of money) is on the line, it's awfully tempting to be thankful if an opponent tanks it and lets me win, but we've all been in a situation, even in a weekend pickup game or a friendly neighborhood tennis match, in which we feel cheated by an opponent who gives up, drifts off, makes excuses instead of playing hard. The most conspicuous version of not giving your best effort would involve consciously deciding not to try because you're going to lose anyway. But if you have developed a temperament that causes you to give up when things aren't going well, even that in a certain sense is giving your opponent less than you should. Respect for an opponent does not mean disrespect for the spirit of competition.

Time-Out for Reflection

- Treating an opponent as an enemy to be crushed is an obvious example of disrespect for the opponent. Can you think of examples in which a superior opponent shows disrespect by only playing hard enough to win? Give examples of verbal remarks, during or after the game, through which a superior player or team might show disrespect for an inferior but honorable opponent.

- Is it ever acceptable to give less than a best effort to conserve energy?

- In an individual sport such as wrestling, is it ever appropriate to let up so as not to embarrass an opponent? In most team sports, does the custom of not running up the score go against the principle of giving your best effort? And what about stalling in basketball when you're ahead?

Avoiding Displays of Disrespect

I owe my opponent my best effort to win, but I should do it in a way that shows my respect for the opponent's effort and my appreciation for the opportunity that the opponent's effort affords me. I should display my seriousness about competition and about winning without displaying disrespect for my opponent. Although good-natured teasing might in some circumstances heighten the competitive spirit in the best sense, as good rivalries do, there's a point at which good-natured teasing turns into disrespectful taunting and trash talking. It requires an appreciation of the particular sport, the level at which it's being played, and the background of the players to make particular decisions about where to draw this line, but it's a line that true competitors need to draw—and that good coaches need to teach them to draw. In fact, if showing disrespect to an opponent is the issue, then behavior that might appear disrespectful, regardless of intent, is disrespectful. In other words, when in doubt, keep your mouth shut. As a general rule, taunting, trash talking, and other forms of behavior that exhibit a disrespect for the opponent have no place in competition, because they display a misunderstanding of the nature of competition.

Time-Out for Reflection

- Would you allow your athletes to stare down opponents? Consider this question in relation to different sports.
- Do you believe it's appropriate to cheer when the other team makes a mistake?
- What can you do to encourage sportsmanship among student fans? Other fans? Parents?
- Is a cocky player disrespectful? Should you discourage cocky behavior? How?

Refraining From "Gamesmanship"

Because athletic competition always involves a psychological aspect, it's not easy to draw the line between acceptable tactics that disrupt your opponent's psychological balance and unacceptable gamesmanship. "Gamesmanship" is the attempt to gain a psychological edge in a manner that is not prohibited by the rules of the game but is nonetheless inappropriate. Gamesmanship shows disrespect for the opponent's effort to play the game well, and it also shows disrespect for the spirit of fair play.

In general, acceptable psychological strategy consists of actions that are "part of the game"—that is, using the skills that the game calls for to put the opponent at a psychological disadvantage. Gamesmanship consists of doing things that are not "part of the game" to disrupt the opponent's psychological state. Rather than using your skills at playing the game to gain the psychological advantage, you attempt to gain that advantage through behavior or remarks that do not involve the skills of the game. To draw the line between acceptable psychological strategy and gamesmanship, we have to know something about the nature and the traditions of the sport. But there is a difference. That it's easy to see the difference between obvious examples of acceptable psychological strategy and unacceptable gamesmanship shows there's a difference. That it's difficult to figure out exactly where to draw the line means that those cases that are close to the line are harder to distinguish from one another—but that doesn't mean that we shouldn't make the distinction.

If, for example, I'm playing a baseline tennis player who loves long rallies, there's nothing unsportsmanlike about serving and volleying in order to end the points quickly. That will put my opponent at a psychological disadvantage, but I'm doing it with the skills of the game. If, however, I repeatedly hold up a server who likes to serve quickly by claiming that I have something in my eye or need to adjust my strings—or, say, if I walk over to pick up the third ball, even though the server doesn't need it and it's not in my way—that would be gamesmanship.

Time-Out for Reflection

- Give examples from your sport of an acceptable way and an unacceptable way to disrupt your opponent's psychological balance. Explain the difference.
- Is it ever consistent with the principle of respect for opponents to disrupt the psychological balance of opponents?

Celebrating Victory Respectfully

Along similar lines, although it might be wise to accept more outward expressions of joy than the traditional Calvinist strands of Anglo-American culture have allowed, celebrations of victory that show disrespect for the opponent, without whom there would be no victory to celebrate, have no place in competition. Or, restated in positive terms, the good sport has to figure out how to express the joy of victory without showing disrespect for the opponent. One traditional answer is to take it into the locker room—that is, don't celebrate in front of the opponent at all. Even if that approach might be overly cautious, it's worth noting that it is motivated by the principle of respect for an opponent. At the other extreme, sticking your finger in the face of the defensive back whom you just beat for a touchdown pass, calling him names that don't merit mentioning here, then spiking the ball right at his feet—this sort of victory celebration (if celebration is the right word at all) exhibits an utter cluelessness about the nature of competition. Your spectacular touchdown catch was only spectacular because you beat a worthy opponent making his best effort. Suppose he had simply stood at the line of scrimmage reciting the alphabet as you ran into the end zone uncontested and caught the pass. Would you have anything to be proud of?

Time-Out for Reflection

- After winning a game or match, in what order should players turn toward fans, friends, family, teammates, coach, opposing coach, opponents, and officials to express joy or appreciation?
- Your team has just won the state championship. Describe how you would like for your players to behave at the buzzer, giving careful attention to the sequence. Describe with as much detail as possible forms of behavior that you would not like to see them engage in.

The Silver Rule

One useful test that might help to make such judgments is to apply something along the lines of the proverbial golden rule, which stresses the importance of attaining a broader perspective and considering the point of view of others. For centuries, the development of a kind of impartiality has been seen by peoples and cultures all over the world to be central to moral education. The golden rule, "Do unto others as you would have them do unto you," expresses, for some, the very essence of the moral point of view. Some 500 years before Jesus offered this moral advice, Confucius probably first formulated the principle in its negative form: "Do not do to others what you do not want them to do to you." Some have called this the "silver rule."

For our purposes, the negative formulation is more to the point: How would it make you feel if your opponent beat you and behaved that way? If it would make you mad, then you need to rethink what you're doing. If you're playing Roger Federer in the finals of Wimbledon, would his falling spontaneously to his knees in a gesture of joyful reverence after winning the last point offend you? Probably not. Or let's say you're playing Serena Williams. Would you be offended if she clenches her fist briefly, her eyes averted downward, after making a beautiful shot, especially if she had clapped her hand against her racket strings a few points earlier to applaud a great shot you had made? Probably not. But what if your opponent runs up to the net after winning a point, or, worse, winning the match, and shakes his fist in your face? Or, consider a situation in which your victorious opponents embrace each other at the final buzzer, and maybe even dance among themselves a bit, and then come over to shake your hands with genuine appreciation for your effort. But what if, right after making the winning basket, your opponents run over to your bench and bump chests with expressions of hostility that call up images of cavemen dancing over a mastodon they've just killed? To say it's all right because you intend to be in their position next time around misses the point.

Sportsmanship on full display at the Olympics

As many parents will tell you, teaching good sportsmanship to young athletes faces many challenges in this SportsCenter driven culture. The attention given to selfish and immature athletes such as Manny Ramirez, Barry Bonds, Ron Artest, and Chris Henry falls far short of showcasing role model behavior.

This is in stark contrast to the refreshing scenes coming from the Beijing Olympics where sportsmanship can be readily seen from both the winners and those suffering "the agony of defeat."

Amid great applause, Dara Torres demonstrated tremendous class when she asked an official to hold up her heat when Therese Alshammar needed to change out suits after a rip happened right before the 50m semifinal event. Torres was very quick to congratulate Britta Steffen of Germany when Torres fell just short of gold by one hundredth of a second in the 50m Freestyle.

Dana Torres is 41 and should be mature enough to show sportsmanship, you say. Then look at Shawn Johnson (age 16) and Nastia Liukin (age 18) openly cheering for each other when a strong performance from one would knock the other from gold medal status.

"I am really happy for her," Liukin said of Johnson.

They are teammates you might argue and should cheer each other on. Then also take note of Cheng Fei of China, along with the Chinese coaches, warmly congratulating Johnson and Liukin after their strong performances on the balance beam.

In track and field, Lolo Jones was in anguish after seeing her gold medal run evaporate when she clipped the second to last hurdle and finished seventh. As she was explaining her mishap she stopped the interview to hug and congratulate silver medalist Sally McLellan of Australia.

"Good job, sweetie," was Jones' message to McLellan.

Reprinted, by permission, from Mark Hopper, 2008, "Sportsmanship on full display at the Olympics." [Online]. Available: http://www.champoli.com/sportsmanship-on-full-display-at-the-olympics/ [May 22, 2009].

Calculated disrespect is worse, but we also have to ask ourselves, whatever the intentions, how will a certain behavior appear? Will it appear consistent with the principle of respect for opponents? It would be nice if all we ever had to do was honestly express ourselves without concern for the effect on others or on the customs and institutions we play a part in, but the nature of competition requires that we think about how we express ourselves and that we develop the depth of character to express ourselves respectfully. The appropriate expression of joy is not an affront to others: the joy of doing something well, of participating in something exhilarating, the joy of winning. But there is such a thing as the inappropriate expression of the joy of victory. The other side of this coin, of course, is that we need to do our best not to misinterpret our opponent's legitimate celebration of victory. Simply because we wanted to win very badly doesn't mean that our opponent's joy over winning is an affront to us.

Rituals of Respect

One final point: We should never overlook the importance of ritual as a way of forming the habit of showing respect to opponents. Think of the postgame handshake, in most sports a practice that is mandatory—not according to the rules, but by custom and tradition. This ritualistic exchange is an opportunity to thank opponents for the competitive opportunity they have provided and to acknowledge their excellence. The coach who understands the principle of respect for an opponent will demand that it be done properly. Look your opponent squarely in the eye, offer a firm handshake—not a wet noodle—and utter one of the customary remarks ("Good game," for example), and say it with conviction. The disrespectful variations of this ritual are of course endless, which means that you have to think about what you're saying. After beating an opponent badly, if you punctuate the handshake with a remark of ironic condescension—for example, saying, "You played a great game," when it isn't true—you've missed the point of the ritual. If boxers routinely embrace after 10 or 12 rounds of trying to beat each other's brains out, athletes in nonviolent and moderately violent sports can shake hands with conviction.

An Example of Teaching Sportsmanship
Baseball—Respect for Opponents

Suppose you are coaching a youth-league or high school baseball team. Here are some things that we've found useful in teaching good sportsmanship to young baseball players. Some of them are based on long-standing tradition, and some we've come up with based on our own experiences.

These suggestions are not meant to be exhaustive, but they are extensive and specific enough to give you an idea of how you might apply the principle of respect for opponents in baseball. In other chapters we'll give examples from other sports to illustrate the other principles of sportsmanship, but we encourage you to come up with your own list of well-known rules, customs, and habits in the sports you are most familiar with that promote the habit of respect for opponents. You can also create sport-specific customs or rituals of your own that would promote respect for opponents.

And, of course, we encourage you to remember that rules, customs, and rituals all require that we make good judgments about their application in particular situations. Like all ethical principles, these guidelines are general. Aristotle says that courage involves hitting the mean between the extremes of recklessness and cowardice, but he also says that courage requires the practical wisdom to see that mean in a particular situation. We offer these general suggestions, then, as guidelines that call for the cultivation of wise judgment.

- Don't allow your players to yell at opponents from the dugout.
- Teach your players that it's all right to cheer when your teammates do something good but not when your opponents make errors or can't throw strikes.
- Have your players shake hands meaningfully after the game. Win or lose, they should take this ritual seriously.
- If you lose, you and your players should offer sincere congratulations after the game. To show they mean it, they should praise the opponent in a specific manner (e.g., "Way to hit the ball!").
- Treat the opposing coach with respect and demand that your players do the same.
- Don't allow players to act cocky.
- Don't allow players to change their attitude or approach to the game whether you're winning or losing. If you're winning, don't allow them to get "chirpy." That is, don't allow them to start laughing and making wisecracks. The same goes for the coach.
- After an away game, be sure to have your team clean the dugout.
- Insist that players avoid displays of emotional immaturity when they strike out, make an error, and so on.
- In postgame discussions, especially with opponents, don't whine or make excuses, and don't allow your players to whine or make excuses. Insist that they accept defeat gracefully, acknowledging their opponents' excellence.
- If you're winning by a large margin in late innings, don't run up the score. You can't ask your players to not swing at the ball or to quit playing good baseball (which would be insulting to the opposing team in its own way), but you can abide by the customs of the game that apply to this situation. Don't hit and run, try to steal bases, and so on.

Wrap-Up

In the end, we are again contending with the two extreme perspectives on competition that we discussed in chapter 2. At one extreme, my opponent is an enemy I try to destroy, for whom nothing but contempt is appropriate. At the other extreme, I make no effort to beat my opponent—I play "just for fun." If we understand the nature of competition, it becomes apparent that both of these views exhibit a disrespect for opponents that misconstrues the very nature of competition. Again, one is too serious and the other isn't serious enough. If I'm so determined to beat you that I can't respect your efforts to win, then I need to remember that we are playing a game; if I'm so lackadaisical about the game that I don't give you my best effort or demand your best effort in return, then I need to remember that I am participating in a competition.

FOUR

The view that we fulfill ourselves with and
through others, that we become who we can be
through those involvements, is as old as the
Dionysian ecstasy, as enduring as the
phenomenon of nationalism, and as recent
as a contemporary coach's exhortation
to his players in behalf of teamwork.
~ Drew A. Hyland, Philosophy of Sport

It's amazing how much can be accomplished if
no one cares who gets the credit.
~ John Wooden

Respect for
Teammates and Team

TEAMMA

Teammates compete not only against opponents but also against each other. Teammates compete with each other to make the starting lineup, to be chosen MVP of the team, to be popular with the team or the coach, to be high scorer for the game or for the season. If winning matters, teammates are necessary and cooperation with teammates is practical, but respect for teammates is more than cooperation.

Ultimately, the most important reasons for respecting teammates are ethical, not merely practical, at least not practical in any obvious sense. I must be thankful for good teammates for the same reason I am thankful for good opponents. If participation in a team sport is a valuable experience, then my teammates make it possible for me to have that experience. No opponents, no game; likewise, no teammates, no team. And, in addition to what I get out of it, I should admire and respect human excellence anywhere I find it. Just as I respect the efforts to excel and the achievements of my opponents, I should respect my teammates' efforts and achievements.

In that sense, respect for teammates is not simply about winning. But an experienced coach knows that a great team requires—even as a pure practicality of winning—a bond among its players that involves deep respect, not merely cooperation. Respect for teammates, like respect for opponents, has to do with how we treat other human beings, win or lose, but respect for teammates also has to do with the nature of a team and of a team effort to win. Being part of a team when the team truly becomes a team, when the team "gels," is one of the great experiences of athletics. It's wonderful to witness it, and it's almost magical to be a part of it. When grudging cooperation—the honor-among-thieves version of teamwork—turns into genuine respect, the results often exceed everyone's expectations.

And, although a team gelling is in part a thing of luck and circumstance—that is, you can't force it—it doesn't happen without hard work. It doesn't happen without good thinking. And it doesn't happen without developing the habit of respect. Indeed, the focus on team cohesion must become a part of every practice, every team meeting, every game, every celebration, and every athletic banquet.

Time-Out for Reflection

- Is it possible for a coach to overemphasize the importance of "the team"? Are there any possible dangers in stressing the values of the team as opposed to values more closely related to individual achievement?

- Is respect for teammates and team the same thing as loyalty to the team? Is there a limit to how much loyalty to the team a coach can demand?

- How do you balance respect for the team with the need for individual creativity and spontaneity?

Why Respect Teammates and Team?

To understand respect for teammates and team, we have to understand the nature of a team effort. What is a team? A team is a group of individuals who agree to cooperate in order to achieve something as a team. In athletic competition, the individuals cooperate so that the team can win. To a great extent, that simply means that each individual tries his or her best. If I'm taking a three-point shot, I do my best to make it. Every basket I make is added to the score of the team. If I can steal the ball, get a rebound, or make a good pass, that contributes to the effort of the team. On this line of reasoning, if we then add up all of the individual efforts of the team members, we get the total team effort, just as we add up all of the baskets that the individuals on a basketball team make during a game to get the team score. And if we turn to team competitions in individual sports, such as tennis, golf, or archery, it seems even more reasonable to say the team effort consists of the sum of the individual efforts.

Let's look first at the team version of an individual sport in which it may be harder to understand what a team effort might consist of. Consider, for example, team tennis—that is, tennis competition in which two teams compete against one another as teams (as opposed to players representing their schools as individuals in a district, regional, or state tournament). If one school plays another in a dual match, that means that the school that wins the most individual matches wins the dual match. If the format is six singles matches and three doubles matches, the school that wins five or more of these matches wins the dual match. Obviously, teamwork is involved in doubles. But leaving that aside for now, the "team" effort, on first examination, means nothing more than how well the singles players and doubles teams play their individual matches. The team effort is equal to the sum of the individual efforts. If our number 2, 4, and 6 singles players win their matches and our number 2 and 3 doubles teams win their matches, our team wins five of the nine individual matches and therefore wins the dual match. Simple math. . .

Or is it? What if the two senior girls on the number 1 doubles team, knowing that the number 3 doubles match was the one that could go either way, had worked with their teammates on the number 3 team all week in practice, preparing them for the match? What if the number 3 singles player after losing her match went over to the number 1 player, who's sulking in the team van after losing a close match, and tells her they need to get over to the number 6 singles match to give their teammate some support? What if one of the lower players, who never gets to play a match but can outrun the number 1 player, lines up all year long next to the number 1 player during running drills, challenging her to keep up? If these sorts of things happen routinely, becoming a part of the team's makeup, if players do these sorts of things because they feel a commitment to the team, not merely to themselves individually, the effects do begin to "add up." Actually, they don't simply add up; they increase geometrically.

As part of a team effort in the fullest sense of the word, individuals become capable of more than they are capable of individually, and the team becomes capable of more than the sum of what the individuals on the team are capable of individually. Now apply it to a team sport, such as basketball, baseball, soccer, volleyball, or football, and this phenomenon becomes even more obvious, but the principle is the same. As the old saying has it, the whole is greater than the sum of the parts. When a team truly becomes a team, in fact, it becomes impossible to speak of summing up at all. We talk of chemistry, of gelling, of everything coming together. We talk of intangibles—we even talk about a kind of "magic."

Time-Out for Reflection

- Have you ever had a firsthand experience, as a coach or as a player, of a team coming together in a magical way? Why did it happen? What factors were involved? Try to be specific.
- Is there such a thing as the negative version of the whole being greater than the sum of the parts? Can animosity, jealousy, and other divisive attitudes among players increase geometrically?

Showing Respect for Teammates and Team

How does this magic come about? There are no guarantees, but it requires the genuine respect of the team members for each other and for the team. If I understand the nature of a team, then I recognize I have an obligation as a team member to respect my teammates and my team. What does this require? As a member of a team, I have a responsibility to play the game and to behave on and off the court in such a way as to contribute to the team's effort to win—that is, to contribute to the team's effort to play the game as well as it can. My excellence as a team athlete, like my excellence as a human being, should make my teammates more excellent. We'll have more to say in the last chapter about the use of sport metaphors to describe life, but suffice it to say here that if I am courageous, self-controlled, and just (to use the cardinal virtues of the classical world), and if I have good judgment in my application of these character traits, my excellence will contribute to my fellow humans. If you look at the stats of, say, Larry Bird, it's obvious he was one of the all-time greats on the basketball court, but much more importantly, when he was on the court his teammates were better because of his presence. And as his presence made them better, he in turn drew from their higher level of spirit and play. You can't calculate it, but you can feel it: That's why we call it "magic."

NEWSBREAK

Excerpt from news conference with NBA star Allen Iverson

Reporter: So you and Coach Brown got caught up on Saturday about practice?

Iverson: If I can't practice, I can't practice. It is as simple as that. It ain't about that at all. It's easy to sum it up if you're just talking about practice. We're sitting here, and I'm supposed to be the franchise player, and we're talking about practice. I mean listen, we're sitting here talking about practice, not a game, not a game, not a game, but we're talking about practice. Not the game that I go out there and die for and play every game like it's my last but we're talking about practice man. How silly is that?

Now I know that I'm supposed to lead by example and all that but I'm not shoving that aside like it don't mean anything. I know it's important, I honestly do but we're talking about practice. We're talking about practice man. *(laughter from the media crowd)* We're talking about practice. We're talking about practice. We're not talking about the game. We're talking about practice. When you come to the arena, and you see me play, you've seen me play right, you've seen me give everything I've got, but we're talking about practice right now. *(more laughter)*

Reporter: But it's an issue that your coach continues to raise?

Iverson: Hey I hear you, it's funny to me too, hey it's strange to me too but we're talking about practice man, we're not even talking about the game, when it actually matters, we're talking about practice.

Reporter: Is it possible that if you practiced, not you but you would make your teammates better?

Iverson: How in the hell can I make my teammates better by practicing?

Reporter: So they can be used to playing with you.

Iverson: They should be used to playing with me. Those are my teammates. So my game is going to deteriorate because I'm not practicing with my teammates? Is my game going to get worse? I'm asking you, is my game going to get worse? So what about my game? Is my game going to get better because other players are hurt on my team, I mean, do that hurt me? Do you think that hurts me? I'm being honest, people are hurt on my team but do that hurt me? Does that hurt me when I go out there and play 48 minutes, does that hurt me as a player? Does that hurt me if this person is hurt or that person is hurt? Do it hurt me?

Reprinted from transcript posted May 10, 2002, at http://sportsillustrated.cnn.com/basketball/news/2002/05/09/iverson_transcript/.

Being Truthful About Abilities and Playing a Role

In order to make this kind of contribution to a team effort, players and coaches must be truthful about individual abilities and weaknesses. Everyone would love to be the high scorer, have the ball 90 percent of the time, hit cleanup, play quarterback instead of center, or "kill" the ball instead of set it. But some people are better shooters than others. Some people can hit a baseball a country mile, and some can barely get it out of the infield. Some people can run like the wind and catch a football if they can touch it, and some can't run like the wind but can knock down a building if it's willing to get right in front of them. Some people were born tall and strong and can soar above the net, and some are short but have great touch.

"Playing a role" is of the essence of team sport. In some sports, the roles are more clearly defined by position; in others, the roles require more judgment and honesty about abilities and limits. If I can set picks and rebound, but I can't dribble or shoot too well, I won't be the next Michael Jordan, but I might be the next Bill Russell. Or I might only be a journeyman high school basketball player making my best contribution to a team's effort to win a 1A district championship. My obligation as a team player is to figure out how my abilities fit into the team's complex set of talents and weaknesses. This includes the best use of my athletic abilities and skills and the contributions of my personality, spirit, intelligence, dedication—all the intangibles of character that can enable my teammates and my team to become better.

Making Individual Sacrifices and Playing a Role

In some situations, the normal roles may reverse, as Scottie Pippen apparently failed to understand in the 1994 NBA play-offs when he refused to go back into the game because the coach decided someone else would take the final shot. The coach figured the other team would be looking for Pippen to take the shot, and he decided to use the star as a decoy—an old ploy that requires the star to understand that his role as a team member is to contribute in each situation whatever will best enable the team to win the game. Maybe Pippen wasn't being selfish; maybe he truly felt that he would hit the last shot and

Seven-time NBA All-Star Scottie Pippen.

that his taking it was the best chance of winning the game. Should he have tried to quickly convey this feeling in the huddle without disrupting the concentration of the team? Maybe. Refusing to go back in the game didn't convey it, nor did it convey his willingness to put his own interest in stardom behind the interests of the team. Now imagine how the guy who's going to take the shot feels when his teammate refuses to go in the game with him? As it turned out, Toni Kukoč made the shot and the team won. A moral victory? Not really.

Respect for the team often involves some form of individual sacrifice. It's interesting that the term "sacrifice" is even used in baseball and softball as a technical term. In certain situations, an individual must sacrifice the opportunity to hit in order to advance a base runner by bunting. In virtually every sport, players are asked to assume roles in a specific situation, a game, or even an entire season—not just because they have no other abilities, but because the team needs them to play those roles. That requires a greater interest in team success than individual performance or statistics. When we say someone is a "team player," we are referring to a character trait: unselfishness. An unselfish player, like an unselfish person, can see the larger picture. In contrast, selfish players think about their own success when they should be thinking about the team's success. In this sense, selfish players do not respect their teams or the sacrifices that their teammates may be making on behalf of the team effort.

Emphasizing the Little Things

At the end of a contest, most players and fans remember who scored the most points, who ran for the touchdowns, who hit the home run, who had the most kills, or who kicked in the winning goal. But in every game there are players who do the "little things" that usually go unnoticed by fans and are rarely mentioned in the newspapers. And these little things are what make possible the "big things" that do get mentioned in the newspapers. These little things are essential for team success, and they should be pointed out and praised by coaches. Such praise reinforces the value of team contributions and the bonds that hold the team together and make success possible.

The glamour of throwing or catching a game-winning touchdown pass requires a good snap, a series of selfless blocks, a running back making a fake handoff look convincing, and another receiver running a pinpoint pattern that occupies one of

Time-Out for Reflection

- In the team meeting after a game, do you mention the little things that were positive?
- Think of the most glamorous part of your sport—scoring in basketball, throwing a touchdown pass in football, spiking the ball in volleyball. Then describe all of the little things that make it possible.

the defenders. And that game-winning, picture-perfect jumper depends on a well-set pick, teammates keeping the off defenders occupied, and someone making the pass just at the moment when the shooter comes around the pick. The perfect spike requires a perfect set and decoy spikers to draw off some of the blockers.

Coaching and Intrasquad Competition

From a coaching standpoint, respect for teammates and team means that competition among teammates—for starting roles, more playing time, or top stats—must always serve the efforts of a team to be a team. Good competition among teammates can contribute to a team effort, but it must be done with that in mind. If two quarterbacks are competing for the starting position, that competition can push both of them to excel, but beneath the competition, their efforts must be understood as a contribution to the team effort. Of course, this kind of competition can be exploited. But if it's nothing but manipulation for the sake of winning, it will often backfire in the long run, and even if it doesn't backfire, it shows that those involved misconstrue the nature of the team. If the team wins and all of the teammates have nothing but contempt for each other because of a coach's ruthless manipulation of intrasquad rivalries, it wasn't really a team that won; it was the coach. Some victories really are hollow.

Team Rules and Team Unity

In the end, team spirit is just that: a spirit. It cannot be manufactured or decreed. But team rules and customs can promote team spirit and team unity. The point of the rules must be clear—namely, to promote the idea that everyone on the team is a part of the team effort and that the efforts of everyone on the team must be directed toward the success of the team. For example, on virtually every team, a rule requiring players to attend all practices and show up on time is essential. Of course, the development of particular rules and customs for a particular team requires good judgment, but such judgments need to be made in light of the principle of respect for teammates and team. Arbitrary rules might create uniform team submission, but not team spirit. In each sport there are many well-known team rules that almost always make sense, but particular teams often call for remarkable creativity in devising team rules that will actually promote team spirit and unity.

And, of course, just as important as coming up with team rules is their use. Nothing destroys team unity more than an unequal application of team rules by coaches or unequal responses to the rules by players. Players are quick to sense when coaches have favorites or play favorites. If you're more strict, demanding, positive, or lenient with some players than others, the others will pick up on it—and resent it. And if some players take advantage of a perceived "special relationship" with the coach, the bonds that hold teammates together begin to break down. When you give special treatment to the star and when the star takes advantage of this special treatment, such unfairness ultimately is an expression of disrespect for the other players and for the team itself. A team effort requires that even though the members of the team differ in athletic ability, their responsibility to the team is equal. Greater ability does not mean less moral responsibility to the team; if anything, it means more.

An Example of Teaching Sportsmanship
Tennis—Respect for Teammates and Team

Because tennis is, in one sense, an individual sport, teaching respect for teammates and team in a scholastic team tennis setting is particularly difficult. But for that reason it provides an excellent opportunity to reflect on what team play is all about. The team concept in tennis is something a coach has to build with great care, and there are many approaches, but here are some suggestions based on our own experiences. Because our experiences are primarily at the college level, we'll use the standard collegiate dual-match format—six singles matches and three doubles matches.

- Explain the team concept to the players. Explain that the primary responsibility of each player is to help the team win *team* matches. Winning the number 6 singles match is just as important as winning the number 1 singles match.

- During competition, require your players who are not playing a match to spread out and watch the matches of their teammates. Expect them to know the score and have suggestions for helping their teammates to relay to you when you walk up to them. Players should be focused on their teammates' matches.

- Teach players to support their teammates. Encourage them to offer appropriate and respectful verbal support between points and to congratulate them after the match.

- Although there is usually no clearly defined space for the athletes who are not playing a match (comparable to a dugout in baseball), require players to sit together while watching matches, not with parents or friends. The support of parents and friends *as spectators* should be encouraged, but interference of parents or friends during competition will break down the unity of the team.

- All players should be required to be present throughout the team match except in cases of emergencies or extraordinary circumstances. Every player is part of the team effort to win the game.

- Insist that all players help their teammates become better in practice. Every member of the team should be willing to feed balls during drills, work with weaker players, and so on.

- Emphasize that the point of practice is not to see who can play the best against teammates in practice, but to prepare the team to compete as a team in team matches. Too much emphasis on playing complete matches in practice (especially a strict ladder challenge system) gives players the impression that beating their teammates is their goal. Emphasize drills that involve the whole team.

- If possible, require players to travel together to and from away matches. If the team travels in a school van, players should not be allowed to take their own cars or ride with parents or friends.

- Never allow young players to seek advice or instruction from their parents, relatives, or friends during practice or match competition.

- During practices and matches and after matches mention the little things that were positive as well as the big things, e.g., players showing support for teammates or helping with equipment. After matches praise lower-level players who won matches for the team with as much enthusiasm as praising the star player for his or her victory.

- Expect all players to conform to the same team rules and customs. The quickest way to destroy team unity is to play favorites when applying rules. For example, if you have a rule that any player who misses a practice without clearing it with you in advance will be suspended for one team match and your star player violates this rule just before the most important match of the season, you must enforce the penalty even if means the team will lose the match.

Wrap-Up

Generally speaking, respect for teammates and team requires a truthful assessment of abilities. In that sense, a team effort requires that individuals sacrifice only their delusions of grandeur. But sometimes individuals may have to hold back even though they have the ability. Respect for teammates and team requires that the individuals give their best, but it also requires the sacrifice of purely selfish interests for the sake of a greater good. In the end, though, the individuals get something back. They give strength to their teammates, but they also draw strength from them. If they're lucky, they have the experience of participating in a whole that's greater than the sum of the parts. It's special; it's magical. It's hard to explain, but it's a powerful and enlightening experience. You can't guarantee it, manufacture it, force it, but you can provide an opportunity for it, and you can cultivate the character traits that contribute to it.

The athlete who understands and develops this aspect of the virtue of sportsmanship will have to contend with teammates who haven't and won't, just as athletes who cultivate respect for opponents will have to deal with opponents who are dis-respectful, but the principle still holds true even when the magic isn't happening. And the magic doesn't happen without the principle of respect for teammates and team. Sometimes virtue is quickly and obviously rewarded, but always it is its own reward. That is, it's better to have it than not to have it. And more often than not, in a team situation respect for teammates and team, even if not directly rewarded, starts to catch on. The high moral ground can be a lonely place, but sometimes it attracts good company.

FIVE

From this fundamental law of nature, by which
men are commanded to endeavour peace, is
derived this second law; that a man be willing,
when others are too, as far-forth, as for peace,
and defence of himself he shall think it necessary, to lay down this right to all things; and
be contented with so much liberty against other
men, as he would allow other men against
himself. For as long as every man holdeth this
right, of doing any thing he liketh; so long are
all men in the condition of war.

~Thomas Hobbes, Leviathan

Boys, the rules don't make much sense, but
I believe in rules. And some of us broke 'em. I
broke 'em. I can't do this—I can't win like this.

~Coach Pete Bell in Blue Chips

Respect for
Officials

OFFICIAL

APPRECIATION

PERSPECTIVE

Respect for officials should be one of the most obvious and least complicated components of good sportsmanship, but there seem to be fewer voices in contemporary sport calling attention to this neglected area than to issues such as trash talking, taunting opponents, or cheating. It's not uncommon for one and the same person to strongly object to verbal abuse of opponents but act as if officials are fair game for any and all manner of attacks. Likewise, it's not uncommon for the same person to consider cheating in sport a mortal sin but treat officials as nothing more than a hindrance to victory. After all, if cheating primarily involves violating the rules of the game in order to gain an unfair advantage over your opponent, and behavior toward officials doesn't directly involve your opponent, then it might seem to some people that one could be scrupulously fair in avoiding cheating while being ruthlessly disrespectful toward officials. But good sportsmanship, as we have already explained, is more than mere rule following.

Imagine this situation. You're attending a youth-league sporting event—it could be soccer, football, softball, baseball, or basketball. The game is close and the competition is tense. The parents in the stands become increasingly loud and boisterous. At some point in the game, perhaps after several questionable judgment calls by officials, the outcome is determined by yet another debatable officiating call. At the end of the game the offending official is verbally abused and literally chased out of the playing area. The irate Little League Parent—the species is not specific to baseball—is so caught up in the moment that he or she yells, screams, and is even prepared to physically confront a youth-league official. This is a depressingly common spectacle in youth-leagues. The game has broken down—the spell has been broken. People who generally recognize ordinary human civility have failed to live up to standards that guide their conduct in normal, everyday life. They have failed to respect officials—they have failed to respect other human beings.

As we have argued throughout this book, the key to good sportsmanship is derived from understanding the nature of what you're doing as a participant in sport. This holds for all participants, even those indirectly involved as fans. The difficulty is that participants are often so caught up in the intensity of the competition that they fail to appreciate those elements of sport that would balance their momentary passion for success and victory. Remember: Sport is both competitive and playful. It is both important and trivial. It depends not only on my own contributions; it also depends essentially on the contributions of my opponents, teammates, coaches, officials, and the traditions of the sport itself. To appreciate this requires a broader perspective. Let's distinguish between the personal perspective of the participants who see things only in terms of their own interests and a more impersonal perspective that involves seeing things in terms of other interests and perspectives. For example, in the moral education of young children, we often insist that they look at things not only from their own point of view but also from the point of view of those who are affected by their actions. We ask, "How would you feel if someone did this to you?" We ask the child to step back and view things impartially.

Precisely the same issue concerning this clash of perspectives is apparent in sport. From my personal point of view as a player, a coach, or even a fan, I am usually most interested in who wins the contest. As a player, I compete against an opponent to win. It is often difficult to step back, as it were, and to see my activity from a larger, impersonal perspective, one that allows me to view it more holistically or completely. Such a broader perspective would enable me to understand and appreciate the role played by and the perspective of my opponents, teammates, and coaches. Ultimately, such a perspective would include an understanding of sport itself in the most general sense—why we play our games and to what extent they matter. As we have suggested—and we can now say this a little differently—virtue in sport arises when we are led outside of ourselves, in the direction of a kind of openness to the broader picture, of selflessly seeing the way things are. And surely an impersonal understanding of sport would include an appreciation of the crucial role played by officials and their perspective, not simply our own single-minded devotion to succeed and passion to win.

Consider John McEnroe's behavior toward tennis officials during his years on the tour. Of course, fans should have admired a good many of his traits as a tennis player: his fiery competitiveness, his creativity and imagination, his deft touch, his stamina. But his behavior toward officials was often inexcusable. His constant complaints about line calls sometimes turned the beauty of his matches into uncivil, shabby representations of emotional immaturity. From his point of view, he was subject to the most incompetent officiating in the history of tennis. From a broader perspective, he had an unreasonably unforgiving view of human error and an unrealistic certainty about his own perceptual judgments. As one tennis commentator put it, if McEnroe had expected the same level of perfection from himself that he did from line judges, he should have walked off the court and quit

Tennis Hall of Famer John McEnroe.

the game. His unsportsmanlike behavior was in part a function of his inability to attain a broader perspective on his play. Even as a mature commentator McEnroe sometimes reverts to the double standard that says officials have to be perfect but players can be human. But, to his credit, nowadays McEnroe likes to poke fun at himself for his infamous outbursts toward officials during his younger years—a clear sign of a broader and more mature perspective on life.

As it happens, we've recently had a special opportunity to experience the role of this broader perspective in sport. One of our good friends has worked himself up from refereeing junior high school basketball games to being the youngest referee in the Continental Basketball Association and finally to being a referee in the NBA. It's an extraordinary experience to attend a professional basketball game after extended conversations with one of the referees. It's remarkable to see the game from his perspective as he attempts to control the game, handle the personalities, interpret the rules, reinforce the traditions, establish the "flow" of the game, and understand the psychological dynamics among the players. It is striking to interpret his judgments and appreciate the depth of his own experience and expertise from a standpoint outside the partisan perspectives of coaches, players, and fans. To put it simply, he's good. The only way to see this, as well as to respect the excellence he has achieved in his craft, is to attain a broader point of view. And, of course, you don't have to be the friend of an official to achieve this perspective.

Why Respect Officials?

The justification of this principle is neither lengthy nor surprising. Since sportsmanship is grounded first of all in the nature of the activity, even our attitudes toward officials should reflect an understanding of sport. In organized sport, officials are "part of the game." They are part of the tacit agreement that makes the game possible.

One cannot have a sport contest without rules and the enforcement of rules; in an organized contest, officials are the interpreters and enforcers of the conditions of competition. Officials are guardians of the spirit of the game. For that reason, respect for officials is closely related to respect for the game. Officials enforce not only the explicit rules but also the traditions and customs of the sport, the unwritten rules. Officials are often the crucial element in a system of sanctions that ensures that the rules are followed. As enforcers of equality, they are there to preserve order. We should respect them for preventing the breakdown of the world of playful competition into a chaotic clash of self-serving individual wills, a "war of all against all," as the 17th-century philosopher Thomas Hobbes memorably described a competitive situation without moral constraints. In everyday life we respect police as guardians of civil order, although we wish they were unnecessary, which, of course, would only come about if we lived in a social world populated only by wholly virtuous individuals. Officials in sport are somewhat like police, somewhat like parents enforcing habits of etiquette and good manners at the dinner table, and somewhat like orchestra conductors interpreting traditions and establishing aesthetic rhythms.

Cuban kicked out after taekwondo disgrace

A CUBAN taekwondo specialist has been banned for life for attacking a referee during a bout.

Angel Valodia Matos exploded during the bronze medal match in the 80 kilogram division. Matos, 31, and his coach, Leodis Gonzalez, were cut adrift of the sport after the referee, Chakir Chelbat, of Sweden, was kicked in the face in an extraordinary outburst.

Chelbat immediately squared up to respond but held his nerve as the stadium erupted. He needed stitches to his mouth.

The ground announcer immediately claimed the action was "a strong violation of the spirit of taekwondo."

Matos was furious that he had been disqualified after taking too much time out for an injury in the middle of his fight against the world silver medalist, Aman Chilmanov, of Kazakhstan.

Gonzalez said the attack was caused by the referee who was too strict in his interpretation of the injury rule. Chilmanov said he believed Matos had a broken toe and would be unable to continue.

Last night the International Olympic Committee said it was satisfied the World Taekwondo Federation had dealt with the matter appropriately.

The federation's secretary general, Yang Jin-Suk, said that as well as the lifetime sanctions, the federation would look at taking legal action against Matos and Gonzalez. The sport is battling to remain on the Olympic program for the 2016 Olympics.

IOC members will vote on sports for 2016 next year in Copenhagen, and there is a strong possibility taekwondo will be removed.

Judo, the rival martial arts sport, is making a strong pitch.

Earlier, a Swedish Greco-Roman wrestler, Ara Abrahamian, was stripped of his 84 kilogram category bronze medal after he became upset at refereeing, which he said cost him the gold medal.

Abrahamian stepped off the dais and placed his medal in the centre of the mat, prompting a strong reaction from the IOC.

The IOC took away his medal and ordered him out of the Olympic village.

Reprinted with permission from Jacquelin Magnay, *Sydney Morning Herald*.

Officials also deserve respect for the same reasons that players and coaches deserve respect. We should respect excellence wherever it resides, and good officials embody the excellence of their craft. Just as dedicated players and coaches work hard to become better in their respective roles as sport participants, dedicated officials are seriously engaged in learning their game and attempting to be as good as they can be. Most officials share with coaches and players a deep love for their sport. Players and coaches should keep in mind that officials, by their very decision to become officials, have demonstrated a significant attachment to their particular sport. Officials aren't cynical skeptics in the sacred space of the play world; rather, they are usually fellow believers in the faith. In short, we should respect officials for their excellence, their desire to be as good as they can be, their love of the game, and their essential contributions to the event in which we're participating.

It is especially important for coaches in youth-leagues, high school sports, and even college athletics to show respect for officials and demand the same of their players. In these situations your role as a moral educator, as a *teacher* of good sportsmanship, is accentuated. Here you have numerous opportunities to exhibit and reinforce habits of civility, restraint, and impartiality. It's important for you to show your players by example that they can love competition and have an intense desire to succeed and win, but that they can do this while exhibiting good sportsmanship.

Finally, respect for officials is particularly important as a defense against the loser's tendency to complain, to blame, to whine, and not to take responsibility for defeat. Coaches should *never* allow their players to make officials the scapegoats for disappointing outcomes. In the moments after a tough loss, you can help players grow as human beings by forcing them to confront their own play in the game instead of blaming officials for the outcome. And you can begin to develop in your players that broader perspective we've emphasized, by suggesting that maybe, just *maybe,* sometimes the officials are right and we are wrong.

Of course, some coaches tell their players that they don't need to be saying anything to the officials because that's the coach's job. That is certainly an acceptable position to take, so long as the coach treats the officials with respect. But some coaches also think that it's their "job" to do whatever it takes to win the game. If that means riding officials until you've got them intimidated, well, that's just part of the game. The officials know that. It might even mean that you say whatever it takes to get yourself thrown out of the game if your team is behind and that's the only way to motivate the team. It goes with the territory. If officials aren't willing to take a little abuse, then they shouldn't put on the stripes.

Well, what is and isn't a part of the game is largely a matter of custom and tradition. And, sadly, the attitude we're describing is probably the way a majority of coaches behave. In that sense—that is, factually speaking—harassing officials is part of the game. But coaches play a part in determining the customs and traditions of the game. What we're asking is that you think about what makes sense—what makes sense in terms of the essential role that officials play in an athletic contest. Without them, it probably won't be an athletic contest for long. What if it became an accepted practice for coaches to take out contracts on officials they didn't like? Would that be "part of the game"? Factually speaking, it would be. But to say it's part of the game suggests that it has something to do with what a game is, that it's part of the nature of an athletic contest. We're saying that it's part of the nature of an athletic contest that officials have an essential function without which the game would not be a game, and that for that reason we ought to respect them.

Showing Respect for Officials

What we have said so far should give you more than a hint of the practical implications involved in respect for officials. But there are some obvious questions that need to be addressed, and we need more specific principles to help us make good judgments about appropriate and inappropriate complaints to officials. Does respect for officials mean that, as a coach, you could never argue, question, or complain about some officiating judgment? No, it does not. The attitude of respect does not necessitate a Pollyannaish response to questionable officiating, nor does it imply milquetoast compliance to whatever happens in the competitive arena. What, then, does it allow?

The Norms of Civil Discourse

There's no reason why relationships with officials should be governed by any other norms than the ones that govern everyday discourse. Respect for an official's judgment is analogous to respect for another's belief or opinion. I should respect your right as an autonomous human being to make up your own mind, hold your own beliefs, and govern yourself. But that doesn't mean I must agree with you or think you're always right. As a matter of fact, if I respect you as a *rational* being—that is, as a being who can reflect about matters and seek good reasons for believing things—it might mean that I feel I have an obligation to respond to your position, question it, test it, and ask for the reasons for your view. I assume that some beliefs are better than others in terms of their support, in terms of their truth; and I assume that you are interested in truth. So I might give my own reasons in an attempt to convince you that you're mistaken. But this should be done with a spirit of civility—that is, with an attitude of respect. I can respect you without necessarily agreeing with or even respecting your opinion. I can engage you in a spirited and even emotional discussion without breaking the bonds of civility.

Likewise, I can respond to officials by questioning and legitimately arguing with their judgments, but I should do this without personal animosity, name-calling, or invective. I should also recognize that some judgments are more appropriately questioned than others. For example, the interpretation of rules is a legitimate area of discussion. However, constant whining about the standard "judgment calls" of an official—the strike zone in softball, offside in soccer, traveling in basketball—is probably not appropriate. Even the response to judgment calls should be guided by the notion that officials are interested in becoming better, so your questions can help them think about and evaluate their performances. But your questions can only be helpful if officials respect your judgment, and continual obsessive complaints are not normally interpreted as helpful advice. In relationships in which we disagree with others, the tone of our response is crucial, and a good sport will seek to find the appropriate emotional hue of respectful, reasoned disagreement.

The Silver Rule

In chapter 4 we introduced the silver rule, Confucius' negative formulation of the golden rule: "Do not do to others what you do not want them to do to you." This maxim is worth considering in every situation that calls for treating others with respect, but it is particularly pertinent in this case. Players, coaches, and fans should keep this simple but profound principle in mind when relating to officials. If you would not want to be threatened, screamed at, cursed, or physically abused if *you* were officiating, then you should not behave in this manner. Broad moral rules do not always generate tidy moral judgments, but the silver rule should be extremely helpful in guiding practical decisions in difficult situations.

The Principle of Charity

In logic and critical reasoning there is an important principle that guides appropriate responses to opposing positions and arguments. If you respond critically to someone, be sure you have interpreted the position accurately and reconstructed the best possible defense of it. Then if you find that there are good reasons for rejecting the position involved, you cannot be accused of attacking a "straw man," rejecting a position or argument that your opponent does not actually hold. This is a principle that encourages impartiality insofar as you attempt to accurately assess what view your opponent holds and what reasons might be given for holding it. An analogous principle might moderate our responses to officials. When responding to or assessing an officiating judgment, you should avoid the habit of continually negative responses, as if officials are *always* wrong. In fact, instant replays on television strikingly reveal how often officials are right and how often the complaints of players and coaches are misguided. A charitable openness to the possibility of the correctness of an official's judgment is an important moderating influence.

Officials are neither always right nor always wrong; however, their very role involves a commitment to impartial interpretation of the rules. There's no reason to believe that they are biased in favor of your opponent, and there *is* good reason to believe that your own judgment as a player, coach, or fan may be skewed in favor of the outcomes that you desire. A charitable attitude toward officials' decisions is a practical and useful device to promote good sportsmanship.

Officials and the Level of Play

A final principle should guide responses to officials in terms of how good we should expect them to be relative to the level of play at which they're participating. The principle is this: The level of officiating should be commensurate with the level of play. There's nothing vague about this principle. There is a tacit understanding among most officials that they must become better if they work at increasingly higher levels of competition. We should expect high school and college officials to be *better* than youth-league and junior high officials. Such expectations will once again act as moderating influences. At the lower levels of competitive sport, we should respond to the poor officiating of beginners and volunteers with disappointed shrugs rather than verbally offensive righteous indignation. At the higher levels, as we have said, spirited discussion is appropriate.

Of course, we can't ignore the fact that there are some bad officials. Put more strongly, some officials may be so incompetent that they should not be allowed to officiate. Whereas I must respect officials as people, I need not respect incompetence, nor must I accept the inability of an official to retain control or maintain the order of the game. Good officials deserve to be praised; bad or incompetent officials deserve a firm but civil negative evaluation, usually by their supervisors. Criticism should always take place within the proper institutional structures, but passive acceptance of the incompetence of particularly bad officials does neither the participants nor the sport itself any favors.

Finally, although our main focus here is the respect of coaches, players, and fans for officials, the implications for officials themselves should be clear. If participants and fans should only expect a level of officiating that is appropriate for the level of play, officials should make sure they are at least that good. Volunteer Little League umpires may not have the time to become masters of the craft of officiating, as we would expect major league umpires to have done, but they have to know the game well enough to officiate a good Little League baseball game. And, given their limitations, they have to do the very best they can, give their best effort just as we expect the players to give theirs. At any level, an official merely going through the motions is inexcusable. Every principle of respect implies a principle of responsibility. In this case, the respect we owe officials implies a responsibility on the part of officials to perform in such a way as to deserve that respect.

Time-Out for Reflection

- Think of specific examples from your sport in which it is appropriate to question an official's judgment. Contrast these examples with cases in which it would be inappropriate.

- Do you agree that coaches should never allow their players to blame officials for a loss?

- Do you apply the same standards of excellence that you expect from officials to your own judgments as a coach?

- Have you ever officiated a sport you didn't know well—say, Little League baseball—because no one else would volunteer and the kids wouldn't get to play otherwise? Were the expectations of the fans about the level of officiating commensurate with the level of play?

- As we'll explain in more detail in the next chapter, one of the most interesting but difficult aspects of sportsmanship involves the unwritten customs and traditions that develop in a sport. Are there different traditions that allow for a more or less spirited response to officials at different levels of play? For different sports?

An Example of Teaching Sportsmanship
Baseball—Respect for Officials

In a sport in which custom seems to allow fans to verbally accost the officials ("Kill the ump!"), teaching young players to treat officials with respect is not an easy task. But there is no other sport in which the integrity of the game depends so heavily upon the judgment of officials and the respect of players for those judgments. Here are some suggestions for how to go about teaching respect for officials for a youth-league or high school baseball team.

- Players should address umpires in a formal manner (e.g., "Mr. or Ms. Umpire," "Sir," or "Ma'am").
- Insist that players be polite or civil when talking to an umpire.
- Don't allow players to argue with umpires—the coach should address the situation.
- Shake hands with the umpires after the game.
- Congratulate the umpire if you think the game was officiated well. (Apologize if you lost your cool during the game, and have your players apologize if they did.)
- After the game, don't allow players to blame umpires for a loss. Stress the idea that acceptance of the human judgment of umpires is part of the game.
- Talk with players about umpires, especially those who are good. Help players appreciate excellence in umpiring by praising good umpires.
- Teach your players the cardinal rule of respect for officials in baseball: Don't show up the umpire! Teach them the customs of the game regarding behavior toward umpires, such as catchers holding a missed call way beyond catching it, catchers or batters turning around toward the umpire to disagree with a call, and so on.
- Have an experienced umpire from the professional or college level come to speak to your players about the role of the official.
- Require your players to volunteer as officials for a lower level of competition so that they will learn to see the officials' perspective on the game.

Wrap-Up

If you've played a sport, you don't have to have a great imagination to see things from the perspective of an opponent or teammate. The perspective of an opponent or teammate is the perspective of another player. And the perspective of an opposing coach is still the perspective of a coach. We've particularly stressed the notion of gaining perspective in this chapter because the perspective of an official is fundamentally different from that of a player or coach.

We've shown that you must understand the vital role of the official in keeping the game a game. But we've also suggested that putting yourself in the official's shoes—either through imagination, getting to know an official personally, or through the actual experience of officiating—is an exercise that every coach, player, and fan needs to go through from time to time.

In organized sport, officials are necessary, but, as the truism of common wisdom proclaims, officials, just like players and coaches, are human. They are fallible. They are no less prone to error than coaches and players who want so badly to win, although, as we've pointed out, they are less prone to errors of bias than the players and coaches. The problem for the good sport is transparent: How do you reconcile the clash between the desire for victory and the apparent fallibility of human judgment, especially when such fallibility (real or imagined) keeps the deep desire for victory from being fulfilled? The solution for the good sport is difficult but clear: civility, sensitivity to another's perspective, charitable vision, and reasonable expectations about the craft of officiating. And we need to remember that more often than not, we find ourselves questioning the judgment of an official because the official has just reminded us of our own fallibility, of our own humanness.

SIX

To enter into a practice is to enter into a relationship not only with its contemporary practitioners but also with those who have preceded us in the practice, particularly those whose achievements extended the reach of the practice to its present point. It is thus the achievement, and a fortiori the authority, of a tradition which I then confront and from which I have to learn. And for this learning and the relationship to the past which it embodies, the virtues of justice, courage, and truthfulness are prerequisite in precisely the same way and for precisely the same reasons as they are in sustaining present relationships within practices.

~ Alasdair MacIntyre, After Virtue

"You guys need to get together and remember what you're doing this for," I said. "You're not doing it for the money. It may seem that way, but that's just an external reward. You're doing it for the internal rewards. You're doing it for each other and the love of the game."

~ Phil Jackson, Sacred Hoops

Respect for
the Game

GAME

The 1995 *Sports Illustrated* baseball preview issue reported the results of a survey of scouts, managers, coaches, and players who were asked to name the players who were best at the fundamentals. Cal Ripken Jr. was the overwhelming winner of the "best overall fundamental player." Tom Verducci, the author of the article, spoke reverently of "players like Ripken, who respect the game and play it soundly." At the other end of the spectrum, as the 1995 NBA playoffs developed, we watched Dennis Rodman (then a member of the San Antonio Spurs) ignore his coach, mug with the fans, and even remove his shoes during a last minute time-out with the outcome of the game still in doubt—hardly a display of respect for the game. Or, consider the fictional world of that wonderful baseball film, *Bull Durham*. Crash Davis, journeyman catcher and tutor of the talented but erratic young pitcher, Ebby Calvin "Nuke" LaLoosh, explains why he dislikes his young, undisciplined pupil: "You don't respect yourself, which is your problem, but you don't respect the game—and that's my problem."

Compared to such basic principles as respect for opponents or respect for officials, "respect for the game" sounds less concrete, too abstract to be helpful in instructing young athletes or guiding appropriate conduct. Yet, as the examples we've discussed show, respect for the game is an important part of the vocabulary of sport. A college track coach we know even describes the behavior of certain athletes as an "insult to the sport." And there is obviously a close connection between respect for the game and the familiar expression "love of the game." Although respect or love for a sport is difficult to explain, it may be one of the most important things you can convey to your players.

Interesting but anecdotal evidence also suggests that many of today's athletes seem to have little or no sense of the history of their sport. Some people may think that it is trivial or unimportant to know about the details of the historical development of a sport. Does it matter whether Ken Griffey Jr. knows who Curt Flood is? Who cares if an NBA player has ever heard of George Mikan? So what if an all-star guard in college or professional basketball is unaware that Bob Cousy's backcourt creativity revolutionized basketball or that Earl "The Pearl" Monroe's spin move initiated an innovative way for a dribbler to change directions? (This move is now so common that you see high school teams using it in warm-up drills before a game.)

Once again, however, we need to call attention to the significance of proper perspective. Perhaps the details, in themselves, are unimportant, but the historical perspective required to appreciate such details is not. A player may believe that a sport requires only an involvement in the immediacy of the moment; in fact, to play a sport is to become involved in a tradition. Rules are created and changed. Skills and strategies develop. Coaching becomes more sophisticated. Playing a sport necessarily involves making contact with something historically larger than the moment. Honor, prestige, and even money may come to be possessed by individual athletes, but they cannot succeed without benefiting from the past insofar as the skills and strategies of a sport have evolved, allowing for such success. In an important sense, the goods related to becoming excellent in a given sport are shared; they are common goods made possible by the genius, effort, and triumphs of a sport's innovators and heroes. The attitude associated with an appreciation of a sport as a historical entity requires a breadth of vision that can affect the way players conduct themselves. Look, for example, at Cal Ripken or Nuke LaLoosh. Now we need to explore more fully why people in sport think respect for the game is important, and how the good sport can display such respect.

Why Respect the Game?

If we return to Cal Ripken Jr. as an example of someone who respects his sport, we can begin to understand what this might mean and why it is important. Ripken grew up around the minor league ballparks where his father coached and managed. He heard the constant instruction in the fundamentals of the game, saw the struggles of the ballplayers to improve their skills, and recognized that knowledge and intensity were sometimes more important than pure athleticism.

Ripken's experience generated knowledge and even a kind of wisdom about what the game demanded of its participants. He became aware of its subtleties, complexities, and traditions. "Respect for the game" is the expression we use to describe this kind of encompassing knowledge and appreciation. In a sense, respect for the game includes the full range of respect that makes up the virtue of sportsmanship. Someone who shows disrespect for an opponent, a teammate, a coach, or an official is at the same time showing disrespect for the game; conversely, a genuine respect for the game necessarily includes an understanding of the need to respect all of its participants as essential to the game.

Cal Ripken Jr., 19-time MLB All-Star.

Underlying all of the principles of sportsmanship we have discussed is the assumption that participation in athletic competition is meaningful, valuable, worthwhile. Why else would we play? One of the reasons we owe respect, even gratitude, to opponents, teammates, coaches, and officials is that they make it possible for us to compete. They make it possible for us to participate in something valuable. The overarching concept that we use to refer to what we are participating in is "the game." And, of course, the game is more than a game. We may have played *a* game Friday night, but by virtue of playing that game, you participated in *the* game. And just as a team effort is more than the sum of the individual efforts of the players and coach, the game is more than a particular game played on a particular day, more than a set of rules that determine how you go about trying to win, and even more than the sum of all of the individual efforts of the countless athletes who've played the game.

No matter what sport we're talking about, "the game" refers to a historical entity, rich in traditions and stories, greatness and great failure, tragedy and comedy, wisdom and folly. If you pick up the bat, you're participating in the same game that Babe Ruth played. You're drawing from his greatness, and you pay tribute to it with your efforts and achievements. There wouldn't be a game without the efforts and achievements of all the participants, but the game is something greater than each of us, and probably even greater than all of us. You can't point to the game in the same way you can point to an opponent or teammate. But you can realize that there is such a thing as the game and that it makes it possible for you to aspire to excellence, to understand something about the human condition, and to develop good character. It is the game in all its complexity that gives us the opportunity to play, and for that reason we owe our respect to the game.

Because respect for the game is less a matter of particular behavior and more a matter of an overarching attitude, the development of that attitude can have a tremendous effect on young athletes. As we have pointed out repeatedly, you must do more than teach your players the skills and strategies of their particular sport. Coaches are also educators of what philosophers once called the "passions" or the "sentiments." Coaches constantly attempt to motivate players, instill desire, generate intensity, reward effort. Coaches perpetually deal with the feelings, emotions, and basic attitudes of their players. Because the development of good character involves the development of basic attitudes, coaches who take the moral education of young athletes seriously must teach them respect for the game.

Showing Respect for the Game

Respect for the game involves an overall attitude toward the sport you're participating in, but that attitude manifests itself in a number of ways. To show respect for the game means to show respect for the rules of the game, the spirit of competition and the spirit of play, the traditions and customs that make the game what it is, and the achievements of others who play or who have played the game.

Respect for Rules

The internal goal of an athletic contest is to win the game. But what counts as winning is determined by the rules of the game. To play a sport is to engage in an activity that is defined in terms of the rules that have been created to make the activity possible. Because a game is essentially a rule-governed activity, the game itself is possible only because of an implicit agreement on the part of each participant to play by the rules. Just as the opponent makes it possible for me to excel, the rules of the game make it possible for me to play. The rules define the very activity we call a sport. Basketball wouldn't exist without the explicit rules that constitute or create the activity we call "basketball." Therefore, there is an interesting sense in which it is impossible for me to play the game, and thus to win the game, by breaking the rules, since I wouldn't be playing if I broke the rules that define the very existence of the game. (We'll say more about this curious issue later in this chapter, since the norms that guide behavior in a sport are both explicit rules and unwritten customs.)

To respect a game is to respect its rules and therefore the agreement that underlies participation in the sport. To play a sport is to seek victory when the game is played, but only within the limits of the rules that have been agreed upon by the participants. For example, one of the functions of the meeting between coaches and umpires before a baseball game is to remind participants of certain rules (e.g., in high school baseball, runners must slide), make explicit agreements if some rules are in doubt (e.g., use of a designated hitter or courtesy runners), and clarify any rules specific to the particular location of the game (e.g., ground rules).

Respect for the game requires an absolute respect for fair play. It rules out cheating—that is, violation of the basic rules that define the sport: how it is to be played, what kind of equipment can be used, who can play, and so on. To cheat is to break the implicit (and sometimes explicit) agreements involved by attempting to gain an unfair advantage over your opponent. Cheating shows a lack of respect for your opponent, but it also shows a lack of respect for your sport, since cheating implies that what is most important is not playing the sport well as defined by its basic rules, but winning—by ignoring those very constraints that make the sport possible. A sport sets up an arena in which an ideal equality reigns: Everyone is equal in relation to the opportunities or possibilities provided by the rules. Cheating disrupts this equality and thus disrupts the underlying conditions of the sport. Hence it is important for a coach to insist that respecting or loving your sport means that a player be committed to the goal of winning, not by any means necessary, but only by those means permitted by the often unimaginably complex possibilities allowed by the rules of the sport.

Time-Out for Reflection

- It is often difficult but appropriate to distinguish between breaking rules for strategic reasons (e.g., in basketball, intentionally fouling a poor free-throw shooter in the final moments of a close game) and cheating, that is, breaking rules in order to gain an unfair advantage over your opponent (e.g., knowingly playing an ineligible player). Examine this distinction by considering a number of examples from your sport. Is this an important distinction?

- During a head-to-head archery match in a single-elimination bracket, one archer's spotting scope falls over in the high wind and breaks. Since they're shooting at a target 70 meters away, without a scope or binoculars it's impossible to see where the arrows hit the target. Seeing what has happened, the other archer is generous enough to call the location of the opponent's arrows. According to the rules, however, an archer may not give or receive assistance while on the shooting line. Is the archer who gives this assistance or the one who receives it acting in an unsportsman-like fashion?

Respect for the Spirit of Competition

Sport is not mere frolic—it involves a contest. In sport there are winners and losers. Some may think these points are so obvious that they need not be mentioned, but, as we've discussed, there are critics of sport who think that competition is inherently bad. They want the conditions of sport changed at various levels in order to lessen the so-called damaging effects of competitive activities. But many of the positive aspects derived from sport are generated by the inherent struggles and tensions associated with engaging in a contest. Because something is at issue when one plays in sport—namely, winning the game or contest—a respect for the competitive atmosphere of sport demands that players attempt to play as well as they can, with intensity and devotion. A respect for competition means that a player must not give up even under the most undesirable circumstances (for example, being soundly thrashed by a better player or team), and a superior player or team should never allow the contest to degenerate into disrespectful festivity simply because the score is lopsided.

Respect for the competitive nature of sport is especially important when teams are mismatched and a team or player is winning or losing badly. Players who respect the game or respect their sport must continue to play as well as they can although the conditions of the contest may be imbalanced. Respect for competition might also come into play when a coach is deciding a lineup before a game. For example, a coach who thinks there is no chance of beating a particular team might

Framingham State women's soccer team receives NCAA Sportsmanship Award

Framingham, MA—The Framingham State College Athletic Department is pleased to announce that the 2006 Framingham State College Women's Soccer Team has been awarded the 2007–08 NCAA Sportsmanship Award by the NCAA Committee on Sportsmanship and Ethical Conduct.

The Rams received their award because of their action on October 29th, 2006, during a Massachusetts State College Athletic Conference (MASCAC) game with the Bridgewater State College Bears. At stake in the game was a postseason berth in the MASCAC Tournament for the Rams and a regular season MASCAC Title for the Bears.

In the 59th minute of play, the Rams took a 1–0 lead as they were awarded a controversial goal by the officials. Freshman forward Kellen Dougherty, who was credited with the goal, and several of her teammates immediately informed head coach Tucker Reynolds and the bench that they should not have been awarded a goal as the ball went through the side netting rather than the front of the goal.

Reynolds instructed his team to inform the officials of the error and after conferring the officials let the call stand and the Rams held a 1–0 lead. In the next minute of play, Reynolds tried to right the wrong by instructing his team to allow Bridgewater State to score and level the playing field and the game again at 1–1.

The Rams eventually lost the game 3–2 and their season ended on Maple Street Field that day, but Reynolds believes the lesson his team, many of whom are studying to be teachers, learned will stay with them for the rest of their lives.

Reprinted with permission from Kathy Lynch, Framingham State College. © Framingham State College

play the weakest players on the squad as a way of showing that the game doesn't really matter. In this case, the coach fails to respect the sport by denying its basic competitive thrust. To seek victory in sport by playing as well as you can at all times may not be the only reason to participate in a sport, but it is surely an essential part for anyone who loves or respects a sport. As we have repeatedly insisted, all of the other reasons you might have for participating require this dedication to the spirit of competition.

Vince Lombardi is often quoted as saying, "Winning isn't everything—it's the only thing." Bart Starr claims that Lombardi actually said, "Winning isn't everything—but making the effort to win is" (Walton, p. 4). Even that remark is a bit of locker-room hyperbole, for, indeed, there are other things that matter in sport besides making an effort to win. But by the very nature of competition, the competitors are obligated to make that effort. Making an effort to win is not everything, but it is an essential part of respect for the game.

Respect for the Spirit of Play

Although participation in sport sometimes involves hard work, sacrifice, and single-minded commitment, you should never forget that sport is a form of human play. Unlike activities with a value that rests primarily on bringing about other valuable or useful things, playful activities are intrinsically valuable. In other words, they are valuable in themselves. As philosophers have said, play is *autotelic*—that is, it is an activity whose goal or purpose is internal to itself rather than external or instrumental.

We choose to play because of the joy, pleasure, satisfaction, or fun of the activity itself. In contrast, we work because we must in order to survive or to live well, so we often fill our lives with hours of toil. Most of us would like to be able to devote ourselves to activities that we would choose to engage in if we were freed from the necessity of working (or, perhaps the best of all possible worlds, to find work that we view as intrinsically valuable). On the one hand, as an activity we freely choose to engage in, play is an arena of liberation and, at its best, joy and affirmation. On the other hand, since play is not an instrumental activity, it produces nothing. It is, in this sense, quite literally useless. Although it may be put in the service of other human values, for example, when it is used as entertainment in professional sports or when it is used to promote nationalism in the Olympic Games, from the standpoint of various worldly matters such as economics, politics, and religion, play is trivial.

Coaches usually do not need to be reminded that sport is competitive, but it is crucial to remind some that it is competitive *play*. Sport is by its very nature paradoxical. It demands that we compete as hard and as fairly as we can, yet that we do this while realizing that sport is play, a set of captivating and intrinsically valuable activities that do not matter in the larger scheme of things. I must play my sport as if nothing matters more than swimming or pitching or putting better so I can win, all the while realizing that it doesn't really matter, from another standpoint, that I succeed. Thus players and coaches must seek to find the proper balance between competitive seriousness and the spirit of play. From the perspective of sportsmanship, understanding the paradoxical nature of sport produces both a sense of fair play and an attitude of generosity and playfulness. If competitiveness is sometimes needed to temper a lack of seriousness or effort on the part of some players, the spirit of play is needed to moderate and guide a sense of competitiveness that may sometimes be too harsh and unrelenting, as if winning by any means necessary is the only purpose of sport participation.

To coaches with their jobs on the line, talking about sport as play may seem out of touch with reality. That makes it sound so childish. Sport is about competition—it's about winning and losing. It's not about Tinkertoys and dolls. Undoubtedly, there are different kinds of play, from the spontaneous running and jumping of children to the more formal rule-governed, competitive play of sport. To say that sport is a form of play is not to reduce it to the frolic of children. To stress the playful character of sport is to appreciate the valuable and even joyful possibilities of participating in such activities, regardless of their value in producing other goods such as money, prestige, honor, fame, or even the momentary satisfaction of victory. From the standpoint of play, what's important in sport is the process, not the product; the activity, not merely the consequences.

Respect for the playful character of sport should produce an attitude that rules out such behavior as taunting, trash talking, and fighting. Think of situations in which small children's play may degenerate and you must remind them that "It's only a game" and that there's something silly about acting as if it mattered so much. Likewise, when players get older, it's often important to remind participants that they're playing *games*, not fighting enemies. One very successful college baseball coach has argued that the traditional postgame handshake between teams should be postponed or even eliminated because the participants need a "cooling-off period" after intense competition. Respect for the playful character of sport should produce all the cooling off players or coaches might need in order to relate to their opponents generously and gracefully after a victory or a difficult defeat. To repeat, if boxers can embrace each other with genuine enthusiasm at the end of a fight, which they often do spontaneously after a good bout, baseball players can shake hands without a cooling-off period.

Time-Out for Reflection

- What are the most significant threats to the spirit of play in sport? Can you distinguish between the threats that come from the very nature of competition and those that come from external sources?

- As a coach, what can you do to instill the spirit of play in your players? Parents? Fans? Administrators?

- As a coach, do you ever set aside some part of your practice for activities that are pure "fun"?

Respect for the Game's Traditions and Customs

One of the most interesting and important aspects of respect for your sport arises because a sport is more than simply a collection of explicit rules laid down at a certain time. A sport is not a static, tightly defined set of behaviors. A sport is a historical entity. It grows and develops. As skills are improved and more is learned, players and coaches develop innovative strategies to respond to opponents. Both teaching and learning your game become more complicated and increasingly sophisticated. Recognizing the deeply historical nature of a sport or game is crucial for sportsmanship, because respect for rules must be understood in the context of both the explicit written rules and the unwritten customs that arise in the development of a sport.

Being a good sport does not require strict, saintly obedience to every written rule. For example, consider this common situation in basketball. In the fourth quarter of a close basketball game, a player steals the ball and goes in for a layup. What should a defensive player do? If she understands the situation and has been well coached, she fouls the offensive player as hard as is necessary in order to keep her from shooting an uncontested layup. The defensive player forces her opponent to make two free throws instead of allowing her to score easy points. There's nothing mysterious about this example. Such a foul is not bad sportsmanship, and it calls for no angry response by the players, coaches, or fans of the opponent's team. Here an explicit rule is violated, but the customs of the sport arising from strategic necessity demand that a player violate the rule. Note, however, that here the rules also allow for the appropriate penalty.

Knowing what is and is not appropriate in the context of the customs of your sport is not always an easy matter. It requires knowledge, experience, and good judgment. To make things even more difficult, customs change. In baseball, at one time it was thought to be "bush league" for a team to attempt to steal bases when it was ahead by four or five runs or more. Now it's more acceptable to attempt to steal bases when a team is considerably ahead, although there is a point, as a matter of good judgment and respect for the game, at which this becomes inappropriate. In baseball it's permissible to steal signals, break up a double play hard at second base, throw inside, and quick pitch; however, it's contrary to the customs of the sport to squeeze when you're far ahead, attempt to injure an infielder by sliding with your spikes high, or yell "Swing!" as the ball crosses the plate during a game. For players and coaches, these matters are directly related to sportsmanship. To say that these actions are contrary to the customs of baseball is to say that it would be *unsportsmanlike* to do them. Only ignorance would excuse a person from being judged this way.

Every sport has its subtleties and nuances. It's important for you to convey to your players that the game has a historical life of its own that they must understand and respect in order to be good sports, not just good players. And, of course, participation in anything that has a historical life means that we must learn and conform ourselves to established traditions while at the same time recognizing—and taking responsibility for—the way in which our decisions, judgments, and actions contribute to an ongoing tradition. How I behave on the playing field today and how I interpret the rules and customs and traditions of the game today will play a role in the creation of the customs and traditions for future players.

Generally speaking, then, respect for the game requires a respect for and adherence to the established customs of the game, but that doesn't excuse us from the responsibility for the formation of new customs. In fact, in some situations the expression "It's part of the game" can become an excuse for behavior that is totally contrary to the very concept of a game. Sometimes administrators, coaches, and players need to step back and make the judgment that something has become a part of the game that shouldn't be. There's no reason, for example, that regular fistfights should be a part of hockey, no reason shouting insults at chair umpires should be a part of tennis, no reason bench-clearing brawls after every inside pitch should be a part of baseball. Precisely because customs and traditions are so much a part of particular sports, especially for young people learning their games, all the participants need to take seriously their roles in the formation of those customs and traditions for the next generation. That may seem like a confusing catch-22 of a predicament; but if it is, it's a predicament humans face in virtually everything they do.

The upshot of what we have said about respect for traditions and customs of a game is this: Whenever you hear the phrase, "It's part of the game," or whenever you use it yourself, you must be very careful to relate it to other central aspects of sport and sportsmanship, as well as to broader moral norms. For example, showboating and trash talking have, as a matter of fact, become a part of the game in many sports. But that doesn't justify the behavior. These actions conflict with respect for opponents, the very nature of athletic competition, and, perhaps more important, the most common, everyday norms of human decency and respect for others. There's no reason to leave behind the central concerns of moral character when we play sports. The truth is just the opposite.

Respect for Achievement and Excellence

One final aspect of respect for your game or sport arises both from its historical nature and from the fact that it is a competitive activity with standards of excellence. When kids begin to play a sport, it's not long before they realize that some players are better than others. Coaches, of course, attempt to teach their players how to become better. It is also important and often humbling for players to learn to recognize real quality in the way their sport is played and to make accurate, that is, realistic judgments about their own abilities and the abilities of others. Such judgments are important not simply because they produce humility and realistic expectations, they are also significant because they generate the desire to develop skills in response to weaknesses in various abilities. But they are also crucial in response to competition with opponents, because accurate judgments about who plays well and who doesn't, about who is good, generate an appreciation of excellence.

As any player knows, losing is difficult. It is often difficult to face our own weaknesses, so we make excuses. We rationalize and we blame. Our opponent was lucky. The officiating was poor. We had an off day. The excuses proliferate. However, a proper respect for achievement requires that I give credit where it is due. When I am beaten by a superior opponent, I should not make excuses and I should not whine. Respect for excellence means that I must accept responsibility for defeat when it is in fact caused by an opponent who played better or *was* better—at least at that time. To respect my game or sport requires admiration (even grudging admiration) for the present achievements of participants.

Finally, insofar as a sport also has a history of past achievements, respect for the game involves respect for those who have played it best. This is the right place for heroes, in sport as elsewhere. Heroes are noteworthy not because of their income, celebrity status, or awards. Instead we should admire them as exemplars of excellence. Appreciation of heroes is appreciation of excellence. They show us what is possible in some area of human endeavor. Recall that we mentioned earlier that coaches are more than simply physical educators: They are also educators of attitudes and desires. Respect for past achievements as embodied in heroes involves opening yourself to the breadth of possibilities in your sport. George Will makes an insightful comment in regard to this concept in *Men at Work: The Craft of Baseball:*

> *It requires a certain largeness of spirit to give generous appreciation to large achievements. A society with a crabbed spirit and a cynical urge to discount and devalue will find that one day, when it needs to draw upon the reservoirs of excellence, the reservoirs have run dry. A society in which the capacity for warm appreciation of excellence atrophies will find that its capacity for excellence diminishes. (p. 329)*

Respect for the game involves the "largeness of spirit" that Will speaks of. We need our heroes in an age of cynicism, and we need to teach our children to admire the good, not merely the rich and famous. Coaches can play a useful role here by stressing respect, admiration, warm appreciation, and other positive attitudes in response to the present and past achievements of players.

An Example of Teaching Sportsmanship
Archery—Respect for the Game

Archery is an ancient sport with long-held traditions and customs. Although there is team competition, for example, in Olympic archery, most archery competition is individual, and most coaching involves coaches teaching individual archers the skills of the sport. Here are some suggestions for how to incorporate lessons on the importance of respect for the game into your coaching in the sport of archery.

- Help players understand and abide by the traditions and customs of archery. For example, showy or noisy celebrations on the shooting line after a good arrow or at the target while scoring a good end are not acceptable. Showboating victory displays are clearly disrespectful to opponents, but they also show that you don't respect the sport enough to abide by its customs.

- Talk about and promote the heroes and innovators of the game. Tell good stories about them. Require the archers you coach to learn about the heroes of the game.

- Talk about the history of the game. Insist that young archers study the history of the game.

- Teach young archers to give their best effort even on their bad days, even if they are outclassed by opponents. Anything less than a best effort shows disrespect for opponents and for the sport.

- Insist that the archers you coach not only love the sport but act like they love it. For example, don't allow them to act "cool," as if they are above the game, as if shooting well doesn't really matter to them. Explain to them that acting cool is nothing but a way of protecting yourself against the disappointment of defeat. It hurts more to lose if you've given your best and acted as if you cared, but there is no other acceptable way to play the game.

- Attempt to instill in young archers a sense of being thankful for the opportunity to play the game. Remind them that a lot of people have gone to a great deal of trouble and expense to make it possible for them to compete.

- Teach archers you coach to help with setting up and taking down the archery field before and after competition.

- Require archers to wear the appropriate clothing as required by the rules—and to wear it in an appropriate manner. The decor of the sport is a long tradition that deserves respect.

- Respect rules. Don't break them yourself and don't allow players to break them. For example, make sure all equipment is legal. Explain to your archers that breaking the rules means you're not playing the game.

- Expect young archers to learn how to keep score accurately and to call arrows accurately and fairly. Contesting calls on your arrows and requesting officials when you know that the arrow is out is a form of gamesmanship that shows disrespect for the officials and for the rules and customs of the game.

Wrap-Up

The players who embody a genuine respect for the game exhibit the "largeness of spirit" that George Will talks about. Respect for rules, the spirit of competition and the spirit of play, the traditions and customs of the game, the achievements of others—seeing ourselves as participants in something greater than each of us individually could achieve, even greater than the sum of our individual achievements—enlarges us. Restricting the ego sometimes means enlarging the spirit.

SEVEN

Rational beings are called persons inasmuch as
their nature already marks them out as ends
in themselves, i.e., as something which is not
to be used merely as means, and hence, there is
imposed thereby a limit on all arbitrary use of
such beings, which are thus objects of respect.

~ Immanuel Kant, Grounding for the
Metaphysics of Morals (Ellington translation)

I had hated him at times during training
camp and I had hated him at times during the
season, but I knew how much he had done for
us, and I knew how much he cared about us.

~ Jerry Kramer on Vince Lombardi

Respect Between Players and Coach

Imagine this situation.

At the beginning of the game a junior college basketball coach tells the point guard not to take a shot without first making a pass. The point guard is the star of the team and the high scorer almost every game, but the coach explains that he needs to get the rest of the team involved in the offense. If you run the offense, the coach explains, the ball will come back to you plenty of times, and for open shots. The first time down, the point guard crosses the line and jacks one up from two steps behind the circle. As he runs by the bench getting back on defense, the coach jumps up and yells at him to run the offense, make the first pass. The player yells an obscenity back at the coach loud enough for half the gym to hear.

Well, we asked you to imagine this situation—but, in fact, it's not an imaginary situation. It happened pretty much as we just described it. And this sort of thing happens all too often. The end of the story is even worse than the beginning. The coach, knowing that the team had no chance to win without the star player, put up with this disrespect. He left the player in the game, and the player continued to disregard the coach's instructions. The player failed to exhibit respect for his coach, and the coach failed to demand respect from the player.

Now imagine this scenario. The high school softball team plays for the district title against their archrival. After three losing seasons in a row, the coach wants this title desperately. There's even talk around town that if she doesn't win district this year, she might be looking for a job. But the archrival has one of the best pitchers in the state. The girls get the bat on the ball, but only get three hits, one of them a perfect leadoff bunt. They advance one of the runners to third but never score. One girl gets thrown out at second on a steal that the coach called. They play flawless defense. Their pitcher throws a brilliant five-hitter, and the archrival scores one run. They lose a hard-fought, well-played game. Back in the locker-room after the game, the coach goes ballistic. She tells her players that they didn't want it bad enough, calls them a bunch of babies. She yells at the player she sent down to second, telling her she's so slow she looks like a pregnant turtle running. "You're pathetic!" she yells, then storms out of the locker-room.

This coach failed to show respect for her players. But in order to deserve the respect that you should demand from your players, you have to treat them with respect. Disrespect for players, as we'll see, can take many forms. Abusive coaches who are more concerned about their own records are the obvious case, but coaches who simply don't care are equally disrespectful. For instance, one of our students recently told us that his high school golf coach would play a round with his buddies while the players were competing in match play, totally ignoring them. In this chapter, we'll first discuss the role of the coach in a team effort, then the respect of players for the coach, and, finally, the respect of the coach for the players.

The Role of the Coach

Just as players, by the very nature of competition, must respect the authority of officials, they must respect the authority of their coach. Authority is the legitimate use of power over others. The abuse of that power sometimes tempts us to believe that all authority is a bad thing, and that we should seek coach–player, teacher–student, and parent–child relationships that are free of authority. The truth is, if you're a coach, you have authority over your players. It can be shaped and developed in different ways, but it can't be avoided. For a coach, just as for a teacher or parent, to renounce authority is to abdicate responsibility. We'll first discuss the authority of the coach and the respect players must have for that authority, but only as a prelude to a discussion of the coach's responsibilities to the players, which, as we've mentioned, we'll discuss in the final section of this chapter.

Part of the authority of a coach comes from the nature of sport. In a team sport especially, many of the decisions, by the very nature of the game, must be made *on behalf of the team* by a coach. If you've ever played in a basketball league on a team without a coach, you know the advantage of having a coach decide who goes in the game and when, what defense to play, or who should take the last shot in a close game. Ten or fifteen people can't make split-second decisions of that nature—they all want to be in the game or they wouldn't be there, and they all were hall-of-fame coaches in a previous life. In that sense, a coach is an integral part of a team effort. The authority of the coach to make decisions on behalf of the whole team is greater than that of any of the players, but the coach's authority derives from the nature of a team effort.

But the authority of a scholastic coach, and therefore the responsibility, is far greater. Whatever the entertainment and financial value of school athletics, there can be only one justification for schools fielding athletic teams—the educational value of participating on those teams for the students. Scholastic coaches are first and foremost educators, teachers of young people. They must understand the place of sport within an academic setting—and that means more than merely keeping sport from interfering with academics. It means that sport ought to *contribute* to the educational goals of the school. If coaches are often granted greater authority over young people's lives and greater autonomy in their work than other teachers (a discrepancy that probably bears some serious rethinking), that should mean not that winning football games is more important than learning geometry, but that coaches have a greater responsibility to broadly influence the lives of students. Simply put, more authority, more responsibility. As we discussed in part I, teachers of all kinds are moral educators, whether they acknowledge it or not, but there's certainly no getting around it for coaches.

An interview with Olympic swimmer Michael Phelps and his coach Bob Bowman

Michael: Bob is—or tries to be a perfectionist. Everything he does has to be perfect or he literally just goes off the deep end. My first interaction—it was right when he came to north Baltimore. I just remember literally saying to myself— "I never want to swim for that guy. Like, he seems mean. I don't want to swim for a mean coach. No way." And then a year later I'm in his group, and that's when everything started.

Bob: I think I'm a little numb to Michael's "wow factor" and probably because I'm always trying to raise the bar.

Michael: He doesn't ease off on the gas pedal. It's just, full speed ahead and if you're not ready then you better get yourself ready. When I was younger, we used to get into it a lot more. I think we've both mellowed out a little bit and I don't get as hotheaded as I used to. I'm a pretty stubborn person. I don't like it when people say little sly comments to me, so we definitely battle back and forth.

Bob: Clearly as we've progressed together, we've become very close.

Michael: We have to be more than just coach–swimmer. We're almost like best friends.

Bob: I don't think either one of us, quite frankly, could do without the other for any period of time.

Michael: I'm not swimming for anyone else. Wherever he goes, I follow. Bob has helped me think that anything is possible and I can swim as fast as I want.

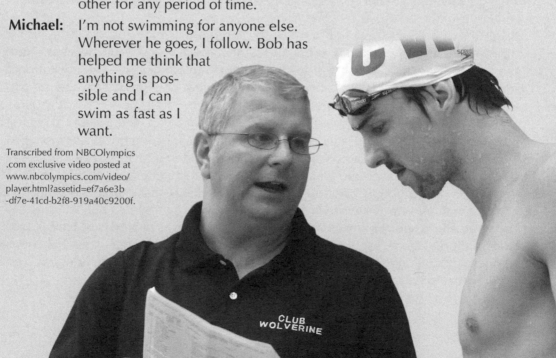

Transcribed from NBCOlympics .com exclusive video posted at www.nbcolympics.com/video/ player.html?assetid=ef7a6e3b -df7e-41cd-b2f8-919a40c9200f.

The Players' Respect for the Coach

Because of the role of the coach, as an integral part of a team effort and as an educator, one of the principles of sportsmanship must be respect for the coach. For some group efforts, freewheeling discussion makes sense; for some, a commanding officer, a leader, a coach is essential. Team efforts in athletics require both discussion and the leadership and authority of a coach, and a sense for which is appropriate when. Just as a team cannot truly be a team without the respect of teammates for each other, without the players' respect for the coach there cannot be a team. They don't necessarily have to "like" the coach, but they do have to respect the coach—which means that they have to treat their coach with respect. Although as a player I may not be blessed with a John Wooden or a Bud Wilkinson, the underlying principle of my relationship to my coach is respect. I may disagree with particular decisions, and I may even express that disagreement, but if I agree to play the game, to be on the team, I have to understand and respect the role of the coach in my team's effort to win.

If a coach goes beyond the bounds of propriety, I may quit the team or even work for that coach's removal, but otherwise, this is the coach I'm stuck with, and my respect for him or her is essential for a team effort to work. Many a parent, and maybe a few athletic directors, has correctly pointed out to a disgruntled young athlete that learning to work with a bad coach is not unlike a good many situations in life. Of course, many a parent has worked to undermine the authority of a coach, and, needless to say, in youth athletics the support of parents is essential. Support here primarily means staying out of the way and letting the child have the experience of playing on a team and playing for a coach, even a difficult one. It ought to be sobering for the players to recognize that the coach is stuck with all of them as well. And it may sometimes be sobering to find out that the coach turned out to know what was what, even if it wasn't obvious at the time. One of the most rewarding experiences for a coach occurs when former players become coaches themselves and come back to confess their newfound respect for the coach who once, supposedly, made their lives miserable. Just as it is helpful for players to try to see the game through the officials' eyes, they need the perspective of seeing it through their coach's eyes as well.

Respect for a scholastic coach is also respect for a teacher. Again, I may not think the world of the particular moral educator I've been blessed or cursed with. We can all cite counterexamples of coaches who build bad character, but the truth is, most coaches, like most teachers, are individuals who've dedicated their lives to the education of young people, sometimes with great reward, sometimes not. Coaches, like teachers, are fallible human beings, but by virtue of the role they've been willing to accept, they deserve the benefit of the doubt with regard to respect.

Of course, the principle of respect for coaches as teachers throws us back into our chicken-and-the-egg educational situation again. If that respect has declined, it's because we haven't taught respect. The upshot of this discussion is that it is the responsibility of coaches to teach respect for legitimate authority in part by

Manuel benches Rollins

Manuel did, in fact, bench Jimmy Rollins in the fifth inning today, two innings after he didn't run out a pop fly that wound up being dropped in shallow left field by Reds shortstop Paul Janish. Not only was it the right message to send at the time, but Manuel and Rollins couldn't have handled it any better during the postgame session with the media. This could've been an explosive situation at the end of an otherwise wildly successful 8–2 homestand. But Manuel didn't embarrass Rollins, and Rollins took full blame for what happened.

"There is no explanation," Rollins said. "I just didn't do it, and sometimes, the manager gets you. I know better. I'll just go out there and make sure I don't do it again. He's the manager, and that's what he's supposed to do. He has two rules: One, be on time. Two, hustle. I broke one of them."

Asked if he was upset with Manuel's discipline, Rollins said he wasn't. "It's like breaking the law and getting mad when the police show up," he said.

Reprinted with permission from *The News Journal* (Wilmington, Delaware) and www.delawareonline.com.

demanding respect for themselves as coaches and as educators. Anything less teaches disrespect. To say that kids now don't respond to authority as previous generations did is probably true, but that means it must be taught—creatively, perceptively—but taught. A part of teaching respect is to teach what counts as treating someone with respect. As we'll discuss in the next section, respect is based in part on understanding and perception, on an evaluation of merit, but it's also partly a matter of habit and practice, a matter of ingrained character. In some cases, treating a person with respect is no longer the reasonable thing to do—in the late 1930s and early 1940s, for example, Adolf Hitler deserved nothing but contempt—but, generally speaking, treating people with respect is a good habit to cultivate.

In this arena, the two extreme approaches to sport we discussed in chapter 2 manifest themselves as *undercoaching* and *overcoaching*. We'll have something to say about overcoaching in the next section. Undercoaching means abdicating the responsibility of authority, restructuring the coach–player relationship so that the coach has less responsibility, especially as an educator. There are many versions of responsible coaching, just as there are many personalities—some of them Bobby Knight–ferocious and some of them John Wooden–saintly—but a coach who accepts the responsibility that comes with the coaching territory must structure the coach–player relationship as a relationship of authority. It may become a friendship, but it's closer to parenthood.

Thus far we've emphasized the need for a coach to *demand* respect. Of course, a big piece of this puzzle is still missing. A coach who doesn't demand respect of the players is shying away from the responsibilities of coaching, but a coach who merely demands it will fail to get it. With the demand for respect comes the responsibility to be worthy of it. When you answer to the first kid who extends the respect of calling you "Coach," you've made a commitment to return that respect. We've dwelled so long on the authority of coaches because the only reason to grant authority to coaches is in order for them to contribute to the education of our children. Underlying the principle of respect for coaches, however, is the respect that all educators should have for the potential of their students to learn.

The Coach's Respect for the Players

What, then, do you owe the players in order to be worthy of their respect? You owe it to them to know and teach the game and to understand, teach, and exhibit the virtue of sportsmanship. Anything less is undercoaching. By the same token, you owe it to them to resist the temptation to overcoach. In other words, you owe it to them to exhibit and to teach the proper balance of seriousness and playfulness that athletic competition calls for.

Knowing and Teaching the Game

If coaches, as an integral part of a team effort, must make decisions on behalf of the team, then they have to know the game. And that means no matter how well you know the sport, you owe it to the players to be a lifelong student of the game—of its new developments as well as its old nuances. We know of no sport that any one individual has understood perfectly. And in some cases, you may have been hired as an assistant football coach, but the school decides to field varsity golf teams and you get the assignment. You know the word "birdie" is used in a peculiar way in the golf world, but beyond that, not much. You can't fake it with kids who know the game, but within the constraints of your other responsibilities, you can make a commitment to learn the game. There's a big difference between walking out on the green and saying, "I'm new at this game, but I'm going to learn it as fast as I can," and saying, "This isn't my main job, so you'll pretty much be on your own." Coaches have a responsibility to know, and therefore to learn, their game. The split-second decision of a coach who is clueless about the game is hardly an improvement on all the players talking at once. Better no coach than a clueless one.

Coaches must be students of the game in order to make coaching decisions based on sound knowledge, and, especially in school athletics, they must be students of the game because they have a responsibility to teach the game to the players. Respect for the players as students of the game, as young people with the potential to learn, means that scholastic coaches are never just recruiters. And, indeed, one of the most exciting aspects of coaching young people is to see them develop as players. Every coach should look in the mirror at the end of each year and ask these questions: Are my players better at the game than they were at the beginning of the year? Are their skills better? Do they understand it better? Have they learned the game?

That's not an easy task, because teaching the game is not an easy task. Some players want to learn, love to learn; some are convinced that they know everything there is to know. Some positively resist instruction, refuse to take seriously the practice drills that develop skills, prefer to look cool rather than poised. Respect for the players' potential to learn, then, doesn't mean giving them whatever they happen to want, because some of them will want to play the game without learning it. The one advantage a coach has over other teachers, though, is that there is a clearly defined goal that all of the players want, namely, to win.

Time-Out for Reflection

- What does it mean to be a "student of the game"? Are you a student of the game? What do you do to keep learning about the game?
- Do coaches have an obligation to attend coaching clinics and meetings in order to gain knowledge about their sport? To read the latest literature on their sport?
- Are your players more knowledgeable about the game after playing for you for a season? After playing for you for several years?

Understanding, Teaching, and Exhibiting the Virtue of Sportsmanship

Coaches exhibit respect for their players, and they merit the respect of their players by knowing and teaching the game. But the responsibility runs deeper than that. If you think about the nature of competition, and about its role within an educational setting, if you understand what it means to compete, you will recognize that respect for your players means, above all, taking responsibility for teaching them the principles of sportsmanship. How? Depending on the age and the character of the players, the balance will differ, but teaching sportsmanship will always involve some combination of explicit instruction, example, and opportunities for practice.

It may seem that there just isn't enough time to fit in sportsmanship lessons on top of teaching players how to play the game well. First of all, if you think about what it means to play the game, then sportsmanship is part of playing it well. But we also want to be clear here: We're not talking about setting aside separate practice sessions on sportsmanship. In talking about explicit instruction, setting an example, and practicing sportsmanship, what we're really asking you to do is to coach in light of the principles of sportsmanship—to run your drills and practices and coach the games in light of these principles. It won't take extra time, and it won't distract from your efforts to win—it might mean that you'll do the things you've always done differently, though.

Teaching by Explicit Instruction

Talk about sportsmanship. Explain it. Don't assume that kids can't understand. Why should you treat an opponent with respect? Because no opponent, no game. Do you want to play the game or not? Do you get something out of playing the game or not? Direct moral exhortation alone is not enough, but in this age of compulsive psychological engineering, it's often shortchanged. Tell them something's wrong or right, tell them why it's wrong or right, and say it like you mean it. Sometimes it's a real eye-opener for them.

When asked what he told his athletes, Brutus Hamilton, the head coach of the U.S. track and field team for the 1952 Olympic Games, said:

> *The gist of my talks with the boys can be reduced to a few simple words, "Honor yourselves, your country, and your opponents with your very best performances and with your very best behavior."* (Walton, p. 105)

Depending on the coach and the situation, saying it like you mean it might involve a reserved seriousness, or it might involve some heartfelt shouting. If you do express anger at players, a good self-check is to ask yourself if you're yelling at them because they lost a game or kicked a ground ball—or because they did something unsportsmanlike. Did they make a mistake or did they do something wrong? If they lost the game or dropped the fly because they made a halfhearted effort, that's an issue of sportsmanship, but if they played the game or went for the ball with all of the skill they possess (that is, that you've taught them), and they still lost or flubbed it, then what's the point of treating them as if they did something morally wrong? Ask yourself if you're really mad at them because they did something wrong, or if you're mad because you didn't get to chalk up another one in the win column. Are you yelling at them to show everybody in the stands that it's their fault, not yours, or to teach them?

Teaching by Example

Preaching without practicing what you preach is better than neither, especially if you're honest enough to admit that you didn't live up to what you preach. But the example that coaches set in the arena of sportsmanship cannot be overestimated. If you insist that the players "behave"—that is, at least on the surface, they appear to respect opponents, teammates, officials, and their coach—but they see you treat others with nothing but disrespect, the lesson is all too clear. What they learn is that when they get to be the one in charge, they can treat others any way they want to. It's only when someone with power over them forces them to behave this way that they should do it, not because it's better or because they'll be better human beings for doing it.

What will players make of your demand that they treat the officials with respect when you repeatedly do the opposite? The coach in most sports may, by custom at least, have a special license to complain to the officials, but a coach can complain in ways that are consistent with respect for the norms of civil discourse, as opposed to complaining in ways that show no understanding of the nature of competition.

What will players make of your demand for respect when, even at the deepest level, you treat them with disrespect? There's no denying that coaches have a special authority over players that players don't have over them, which means that coaches must sometimes make decisions that are unpopular with the players. But the question still remains: Do you exercise your authority in ways consistent with respect for your players as students of the game and of life, as fellow human beings, as kids with the potential to learn? On this score, we recommend the proverbial conversation with the mirror after every practice and every game. The appropriate question: What did my behavior teach them about sportsmanship?

Practicing Sportsmanship

If sportsmanship is a virtue, it can be practiced. Coaches have a responsibility to make the workouts as well as the games occasions for the practice of sportsmanship. Every good coach knows that even though an occasional light workout is a good idea, generally speaking, halfhearted efforts in daily practices will become a habit of halfheartedness that translates into halfhearted efforts in competition. Likewise, even though occasionally allowing players to let off steam in practice is probably a good idea, if you allow your players to show disrespect for opponents, teammates, or the game in daily practice you'll find that they have developed the habit of disrespect. If it's OK for them to throw their rackets when they're playing a teammate in a practice match, then how could it not be OK to do it during a match? Even if it's not OK, it's a tough habit to break. Not many people know that when Björn Borg started playing tennis as a teenager in Sweden, he had a bad temper. After one outburst on the court, his coach sent him home for a couple of weeks and told him that when he came back, one more episode would result in a permanent expulsion from the tennis club. As most people know, no tennis player in the history of the game has conducted himself with greater dignity than Björn Borg did during his career.

Hall of Fame tennis player Björn Borg.

Time-Out for Reflection

- Is the teaching of sportsmanship a part of your coaching? What are the specific ways in which you reinforce the value of sportsmanship?

- Do you discuss issues of sportsmanship with your players? At the beginning of the season? When the occasion calls for it? When stories hit the news about famous athletes acting in a particularly sportsmanlike or unsportsmanlike fashion, do you discuss these events with your players?

- In what ways do you set a good example for sportsmanlike behavior? In what ways do you set a bad example?

- Do you allow unsportsmanlike behavior in practice that you wouldn't allow in a game? What do you do in practice to help your players develop the habit of respect for others and for the game?

Resisting the Temptation to Overcoach

Sometimes the expression "student-centered education," especially at the college level where recruitment and retention of students pay the bills, means giving students whatever they want, as if they are customers of a business or consumers of a product. If consumers want cars with bright colors, who are we to question their judgment? Educating students and manufacturing cars, however, are not the same thing. Respect for the potential of young athletes to learn doesn't mean letting them do whatever they want. It necessarily means making a good many decisions for them, decisions that may not be popular, at least at the time. Otherwise, it makes no sense to say that teachers teach students.

But there is a great danger that we will forget the purpose of making these decisions. Education is an inescapably paternalistic undertaking—that is, it involves teachers making decisions on behalf of students—but it is a paradoxical sort of paternalism. To some extent, it always involves making decisions for students, but the purpose of this paternalism is to *educate* them—that is, to bring them to the point at which they can make responsible decisions for themselves. The goal of educational paternalism, like the goal of parental paternalism, is eventually to make itself superfluous.

The tremendous amount of authority that is typically vested in coaches makes it easy for coaches to forget the ultimate goal of this authority. The primary reason for the existence of a scholastic athletic program is the education of young athletes. If you forget that, you can easily come to think that you have this special authority because you're the one who ultimately matters, that the whole team exists for your sake. Then you start to make decisions for the team that will serve your own ends—to advance your own career, to impress local boosters, to inflate your ego. If you do a good job, your career ought to advance, local boosters ought to be impressed, and you should be proud of your accomplishments. It bears mentioning, however, that there is a difference between being proud and being egotistical.

Simply put, the coach can become more important than the players. It's interesting to note the way in which so many of the rule changes of the past few decades, especially in college sports, have made the coach increasingly more important, to the extent that in big-time college athletics the coach often becomes the focus of the whole enterprise. The winning-is-everything attitude very often is related to the overemphasis on the importance of the coach. All too often, for the coach, winning is the sole yardstick of worth. Job, salary, prestige—the win column for the coach has repercussions beyond the playing field. The mirror check on this issue: Am I here for the players as their coach and teacher, or are they here for me? Am I teaching them or exploiting them?

One of the results of overemphasis on the importance of the coach is the temptation to overcoach. If your record, your career, or your ego becomes the focus of your effort, then it's tempting to make all the decisions for the players, to provide all of the energy and spirit—even if it's the spirit of fear. If your win–loss record is all-important, then you're going to make sure that everything gets done that needs to get done, whether your doing it is in the best interest of the players' education or not. But if you remember that the ultimate purpose is to help your players grow into autonomous adults, at some point you have to let them make the decisions, make the mistakes, make what you've taught them their own. Somewhere along the line, you have to recede as a teacher of the game, you have to fall back into your role as the coach who is an integral part of a team effort, and you have to let them play the game. It is revealing that we talk about the win–loss records of coaches when in fact, strictly speaking, coaches don't win or lose; teams do. Coaches coach, and, strictly speaking, the players play the game.

Exhibiting and Teaching the Proper Balance of Playfulness and Seriousness

In effect, then, you demonstrate respect for your players by exhibiting the proper balance of playfulness and seriousness in your own behavior. Coaches who don't take the responsibilities of coaching seriously enough undercoach; coaches who take themselves too seriously, who place too much importance on themselves and not enough on the education of the players, overcoach. Like parents, coaches can err in both directions. You can become so accommodating, similar to car manufacturers responding to market trends, that you abdicate your responsibility; and you can become so authoritarian that you abuse the legitimate authority vested in you.

In finding this balance, you must be truthful about yourself, specifically, about your own abilities and limitations. Different people will, and should, find different ways of handling the responsibilities of coaching, of showing respect for the players. Some coaches are going to be more playful than others, and some more serious than others. But the basic principle of finding a proper balance is still the goal. During the mirror checks, some coaches need to say "Lighten up," and others, "Get serious."

For those who need to lighten up, one way to gain perspective on this balance is to view sport in relation to the rest of life, as we'll discuss in chapter 9. To the athletes on the playing field, the game is everything, and seriousness about competition requires that we don't step on the field unless we intend to give it all we've got. At the same time, we'd do well to consider the outcome of a high school football game or swimming meet alongside, say, the death of several thousand innocent people in the terrorist attack on the World Trade Center, scientists trying to discover a cure for cancer, teenagers dying in drive-by shootings in cities all over the nation, and thousands driven from their homes, tortured, raped, and murdered in Darfur. Sport isn't everything. It's a game. It's an avenue to some very important things for many people, but there are other avenues.

An Example of Teaching Sportsmanship
Basketball—Respect Between Players and Coach

In some sports, the coach prepares athletes for competition but isn't an active participant in the competition. In basketball, the coach and players practice together and compete together, and the example that some professional basketball superstars have set makes it especially difficult to teach respect between players and coach in this sport. The roles must be clearly defined. Respect must be given and earned, but it also must be taught. Here are a few suggestions for how to go about teaching respect between players and coach for a youth-league or high school basketball team.

- Tell the players specifically how they may address you. "Coach" is highly recommended; calling you by your first name is not. It shows their acceptance of your role, and, of course, it commits you to live up to being their coach.

- Expect players to listen carefully to your instructions. In team meetings and during practices, don't allow players to talk while the coach is talking.

- Be clear about who makes the various decisions on the team. It is the coach, for example, who chooses the starters and makes player substitutions, not the players, parents, or fans.

- Use an appropriate model or analogy to explain how you understand your authority and the responsibilities of the players. For example, you might suggest that your players treat you as they would a parent or a respected teacher.

- Be specific about little signs of disrespect that will not be tolerated: eyes rolling, moping, lack of hustle, questioning decisions at inappropriate times, and so on.

- Show players that you respect them by expecting mature behavior from them and by treating them, as much as possible, as adults who are capable of understanding your and their roles on the team.

- Reserve some time during the season to talk to each player individually. Talk about how the player thinks things are going on the team. Ask for suggestions and discuss them.

- Exhibit the principles of sportsmanship in your own behavior, and teach them the principles of sportsmanship through example and explicit instruction and by developing practice routines that instill the character traits of sportsmanship.

- When you talk about sportsmanship, make connections to life beyond the basketball court. In other words, make it clear to your players that the character they are building in the gym should carry over into the rest of their lives.

- Don't forget that your players need to have fun. Reserve some practice time for drills or activities that are strictly for fun.

Wrap-Up

The relationship between coach and players is special. Depending on the personalities, the age of the players, and the particular sport, that relationship can take many forms. But what we've tried to argue in this chapter is that the foundation of that relationship must be reciprocal respect. That respect, like the respect for opponents, teammates, and officials, is based on the nature of athletic competition and the role that the coach plays in a team effort. And, because the coach in a scholastic setting is an educator in the broadest sense of the word, the responsibility for building this relationship of respect is even greater.

PART III

Thinking About Sport and Life

EIGHT

Yet notoriously the cultivation of truthfulness, justice and courage will often, the world being what it contingently is, bar us from being rich or famous or powerful. Thus although we may hope that we can not only achieve the standards of excellence and the internal goods of certain practices by possessing the virtues and become rich, famous and powerful, the virtues are always a potential stumbling block to this comfortable ambition. We should therefore expect that, if in a particular society the pursuit of external goods were to become dominant, the concept of the virtues might suffer first attrition and then perhaps something near total effacement, although simulacra might abound.

~ Alasdair MacIntyre, After Virtue

Sport, Society, and Education

SOCIET

In the final part of this book, we want to raise again some of the questions that arose in the first chapter. We can view sport in two very different ways. We can focus on the very nature of sport, as we have done in attempting to ground the virtue of sportsmanship and the principles of respect in the nature of the various activities that we refer to as "sport." Here we focus on what is typical of sporting activities: that they are rule-governed, competitive, and inherently valuable; that they involve contests in which persons come together in a mutual quest for excellence; that they involve customs and traditions that embody standards of excellence. In this sense we may speak of the "world" of sports, or the world of a particular sport, or a play world created by the arbitrary invention of the constitutive rules of a sport. Within this ideal world, space and time are set off from the ordinary world, meanings and purposes are transparent, and values internal to this world are shared—victory, achievement, excellence, hard work, perseverance, courage in the face of possible failure, and more.

Sport as a Microcosm

But from another perspective, the play world or the sports world is far from pure. It is a commonplace to speak of sport as a microcosm, which seems to imply that it mirrors or represents the larger world. But this is ambiguous. When we attempt to isolate the world of sports, as described in the previous paragraph, we may be impressed by the internal qualities of sport, by the way the rules create an ideal space within which a kind of absolute justice prevails.

If "life is unfair" outside the world of sports, we may prefer a reality within which the strike zone is determinate, the hoop is always 10 feet above the ground, and if you stay in your lane you win the race, regardless of race, class, gender, or ethnicity (ignore for the moment the ways in which sports may be revised in order to ensure equal opportunity or justice across the barriers of sex, for example). But this is not the typical way in which people interpret the notion of sport as a microcosm. In contrast to an isolationist interpretation of the microcosm of sport, a more contextualist approach generates a very different view or at least a perspective that tends to emphasize different elements of contemporary sport. According to this interpretation, sport is very much a social phenomenon that represents or dramatizes elements of our larger social life. Hence, given the contexts in which contemporary sport is played, it is not surprising for people to raise questions related to race, gender, nationalism, and economic matters—and to be concerned about the effect of sport on the rest of our society.

The isolationist and contextualist approaches to sport are not mutually exclusive. Of course sport inevitably will be influenced by larger social realities. Of course it is important for sociologists, historians, and economists to help us understand the ways in which the development of sport represents controversial aspects of our social life. The danger, however, is to focus exclusively on various kinds of contingent social or economic facts and ignore the ways in which these factors contaminate or taint the internal reality of sport.

When we look at "contemporary sport," what do we see? But, even that expression can be misleading. Should we look at the NFL, or *Friday Night Lights*—at least before ESPN decided to broadcast Friday-night college football games? No wonder the critics of contemporary sport raise their voices in response to what they see: cheating, performance-enhancing drugs, aggression, selfishness, out-of-control salaries, disrespectful egotistic displays. What are our children really learning from the highly commercial world of sport? Is life really all about winning? Making enormous sums of money? Acting as if you and your game are the center of the universe? Maybe we should ban sports as hypercompetitive activities that contribute to alienation, aggression, and materialism.

In *Sport,* Colin McGinn makes an apt comment on these disturbing aspects of sport:

> *My reply to these natural misgivings is simple: what we are describing is the corruption of sport, not its essence. Yes, the sporting impulse—the sporting spirit, we might say—has been corrupted and debased; but this is not intrinsic to the very nature of sport. It's an imposition from outside, from extraneous sources. The problem, simply put, is money: capitalism, commercialization. Do you think sex should be banned? Do you think sex is an inherently bad thing? I certainly hope not. . . . But sex also has been corrupted, by money, by capitalism, by commercialization. Indeed, you might say that sex has always been corrupted, one way or another, without being corrupt. People see ways to make money out of sex—by pornography, prostitution, and sexual slavery—and so they corrupt it. . . . But it isn't that sex is in itself a bad thing: corruption isn't part of its very nature. Almost any worthwhile thing can be corrupted when money becomes involved (think of the big-time art market or day-to-day politics). Sport has accordingly become corrupted in our money-driven society, deformed and defiled. (McGinn, p. 119)*

McGinn's analysis provides a helpful way of considering issues related to sport and society. There is the thing itself, and there are various factors that may contaminate or corrupt it. There is an activity whose nature or essence may be isolated and made the object of attention (at least for purposes of analysis), and there are nonessential or atypical factors that infect the activity. The TCU receiver and the division II softball player described in the introduction saw themselves as participating in an activity defined by rules, grounded in tacit agreements, and guided by notions of just desserts and generosity, values that are internal to the sports in question. They seemed relatively uninterested in the economic consequences of losing—as well they should. On the other hand, when athletes call themselves entertainers, when it's all about winning, and championships, and marketing oneself, when it's all about gaining an edge by whatever means possible, then the activities in question have been reduced to market transactions, or warlike confrontations, or unbridled expressions of self-assertion. If there is an ethical climate surrounding contemporary, commercialized sport, and such a climate leads to the negative things that are so prevalent, then it is all the more important to refocus our attention on sport in its uncorrupted form as the basis for taking seriously the possibility of sportsmanlike behavior and the development of a wide range of habits associated with good sportsmanship.

Sports Heroes and Role Models

One other aspect of sport, society, and education involves the exalted status that celebrated athletes have in our society. An important issue was central to a well-known public dispute between former NBA players Karl Malone and Charles Barkley: Are famous athletes role models? Do they have special responsibilities because people, especially children, look up to them and strive to imitate them? Barkley says this: "I'm not a role model. . . . The ability to run and dunk a basketball should not make you God Almighty. There are a million guys in jail who can play ball. Should they be role models? Of course not" (Wellman, p. 331). To this, Malone responds, "Charles, you can deny being a role model all you want, but I don't think it's your decision to make. We don't choose to be role models, we are chosen. Our only choice is whether to be a good role model or a bad one" (Wellman, p. 331).

The dispute is especially interesting because it crystallizes some of the issues raised in this chapter. In order to see why Barkley and Malone may be arguing at

NBA Hall of Famer Charles Barkley.

cross-purposes and how the dispute relates to our previous discussion it's important to make some distinctions. First, let's distinguish two distinct senses of being a role model. In one sense, a person is a role model if he or she is, in fact, imitated by someone. In another sense, a person is a role model if he or she is *worthy* of being imitated. For example, a child may in fact imitate a parent, quite apart from the question of whether the parent ought to be imitated or should be a model for the child's behavior. A young boy may imitate the behavior of his father, who happens to be a bad person, or fail to imitate the more admirable qualities of his mother. Note the ambiguity of asking, "Are parents role models?"—an ambiguity that is analogous to asking, "Are celebrated athletes role models?" In the descriptive sense, we might respond, "Of course!" In a normative sense, we might say, "Not necessarily."

Also, a person may be a role model in either sense in a relatively narrow aspect of life or in a more general sense, throughout all areas of life. For example, a child may imitate the behavior of a successful parent in some profession, modeling behavior as an apprentice might. Or a child may be influenced by a key mentor in becoming a good lawyer, teacher, physician, or plumber while recognizing that good plumbers may not be good people, generally speaking, and a good lawyer may also be selfish, cynical, and abusive. So when we wonder whether a person is a role model, we may be wondering whether that person is worthy of being imitated in some role or whether that person is an admirable human being overall.

Once we make these distinctions, it seems clear that Barkley and Malone are focusing on different things. Barkley claims that there's nothing intrinsic to sports participation that qualifies the athlete for being a role model in the broader sense. There's nothing intrinsic to being a sports hero that merits the status of being a moral exemplar, like Socrates, Confucius, Jesus, or your grandmother. He's probably right about this. However great an athlete is at playing a sport, it's not clear that he or she is a good person, period. And a plausible explanation for this is not hard to find. Given the contaminated nature of commercialized contemporary sport, the external pressures involved, and the seemingly widespread lack of focus on what we have called the internal values of sport, it's no wonder we see in the lives of many celebrated athletes a flimsy connection between great athletic achievements and good moral character, more broadly speaking.

In contrast to Barkley, who seems to be relatively unconcerned about the fact that celebrated athletes *are* imitated, Malone seems to focus exclusively on the fact that our sports heroes are influential and that athletes therefore have special responsibilities because of their heightened influence on the conduct of others. And he may be right about this, but his defense (as well as that of many others who find the role-model argument so persuasive) focuses on the more general sense of being a role model—that is, a moral exemplar. So we find that some coaches, at different levels, stress the importance of good works in the community or require service activities, and some sports heroes stress the importance of "giving back" to the community. Now, all of this may be appropriate and beneficial, yet it seems to mislead or turn our attention away from the arena within which celebrated athletes obviously have the most influence. The public may or may not become aware of the social contributions of a famous athlete. Likewise, we may become disheartened when we find out that the athlete who worked at the soup kitchen was arrested later in the day for . . . (you fill in the blank).

In many cases, we know very little about the lives of our sports heroes outside the arena of athletic competition. That's where we see them, admire their achievements, and appreciate the qualities that contribute to their quest for excellence. That's where they are most influential. Independent of the question of whether they are admirable human beings in general, celebrated athletes are role models in a narrow sense, in the sense that the way they behave in their role as athletes has an influence on others, especially younger aspiring athletes. It's interesting that Karl Malone became the most well-known spokesman for the view that athletes are "role models," yet he had the reputation of being a dirty basketball player, a thug on the court. If he was so concerned about the heightened influence that our sports heroes have on the moral education of others, he should have been much more concerned about the way he played basketball instead of focusing on the message he sent by being a good guy off the court.

Barkley's view underplays the fact that celebrated athletes can influence others, but it rightly points out that there is no necessary connection between being a great athlete and being a good person. Malone's view correctly insists that athletes can have a special influence on others, but it misplaces the locus of that heightened influence. We should expect our sports heroes to be good people, but not because they are famous. We should hope that all people recognize their responsibilities to encourage virtue and discourage vice and to be especially sensitive to the way their conduct and attitudes may influence children. Famous athletes do have special responsibilities, however, to conduct themselves well in their roles as athletes. That's the place where their influence is greatest, and that's where, paradoxically, their conduct has the best chance of being educational in the broader sense.

Are celebrated athletes role models? Yes, descriptively but narrowly, and the narrower focus may be most important for moral education in the broader sense,

Time-Out for Reflection

- Who are some of the athletes that you think of as role models? How much of that has to do with their athletic prowess and how much has to do with character traits that you admire and would like for young people to emulate?

- For athletes that you would consider role models, how much of your admiration stems from their sportsmanlike conduct on the playing field or court and how much stems from their good works outside the sports arena?

- What are the traits in athletes that you think would make them *worthy* of being role models?

for helping younger sport participants to develop habits of respect that will extend beyond sport. The fact that we may admire athletic achievement but not the athlete isn't a reflection of sport itself; it's a reflection of its corruption. Would that our sports heroes exhibited respect for opponents, teammates and team, officials, coaches, and the very games they play, and that they talked about the centrality of sportsmanship in interviews and other public situations. Their most obvious responsibilities as role models involve their contributions to the practice of good conduct in sport.

The Culture of Disrespect

As we discussed earlier in this chapter, it's possible to think of sport as a microcosm of the larger society because of a correlation between the two. Especially when we look back over the last few decades we see a direct correlation between changes in our sports culture and changes in our broader culture. This is a book about the nature of sport and sportsmanship, a defense of sportsmanship, and we don't claim to be sociologists. But it's impossible not to notice some disturbing parallels between the decline of civility in our overall public discourse and the decline of civility in our sports culture. It's doubtful that even the best empirical research will be able to tell us exactly what is causing what, and we should always be cautious about making the leap from correlation to cause.

However, it seems likely that the causal connection in this case runs both directions. We've talked about the corrupting influence of commercialism on sport. How could the greater cultural trends in our society not flow into the sports world? And we've talked about the thorny issue of treating sports figures as role models. How could the conduct of famous athletes who are idolized by our children not influence the way they behave? Just look at the sports paraphernalia that so many young people adorn themselves with, and it's clear that they dream of becoming their sports heroes. Just look at their mannerisms, listen to the way they talk, and you can see them imitating the icons of our commercial culture—movie stars, rock stars, and sports heroes.

Many commentators have talked in recent years about the lack of civility in our public discourse. This cultural trend runs the gamut from the vicious attack ads and negative campaigning in the political arena to the downright nastiness of talk radio and TV to the shouting matches of cable news. Certainly, we can still witness acts of genuine civility and selfless generosity if we pay attention, but it would hardly be an exaggeration to claim that a dominant trend in our society has been in the direction of a culture of disrespect. And although we occasionally witness remarkable acts of sportsmanship from great athletes, as we've tried to document with some of our Newsbreaks, it would not be an exaggeration to describe what's going on in the sports world, especially professional sport, as a culture of disrespect.

In fact, it's almost a perverse reversal—in a culture of disrespect, you get respect by being in-your-face disrespectful. In an early scene in Lawrence Kasdan's 1992 movie *Grand Canyon,* Mack, a suburbanite played by Kevin Kline, takes a wrong turn and ends up in a desolate and dangerous part of East Los Angeles late at night. His car breaks down, and he finally manages to locate someone with a tow truck who's willing to drive into that part of town—Simon, a character played by Danny Glover. When Simon arrives, a gang of young thugs is about to rob, maybe kill, the suburbanite. After a touch-and-go negotiation with the gang leader, Simon finally convinces him to let Mack and him go.

But the street kid wants Simon to answer a question: "But first you gotta answer one more thing for me, and you gotta tell me the truth. Are you askin' me a favor as a sign of respect . . . or are you askin' me a favor 'cause I got the gun?" Simon answers, "Man, the world ain't supposed to work like this. I mean, maybe you don't know that, but this ain't the way it's supposed to be. I'm supposed to be able to do my job without asking you if I can. That dude is supposed to be able to wait with his car without you rippin' him off. Everything's supposed to be different than what it is."

The gang leader insists: "So what's your answer?" Simon answers: "You don't have the gun, we ain't havin' this conversation." And the young thug says: "That's what I thought. No gun, no respect. That's why I always got the gun."

OK, only a few prominent athletes try to get respect by carrying a gun, but the point of this scene is that in the street culture the gang leader grew up in, you get respect not by having good character but by being tough, aggressive, combative—in other words, disrespectful. Danny Glover's character tells the gang leader that this isn't the way the world is supposed to be, but it just doesn't register. Call it street culture, prison culture, or Wall Street culture, the culture of disrespect is alive and well and thriving outside of East LA. It's on our football fields and basketball courts and tennis courts, and it's on our televisions and radios and in our political discourse.

How did this culture of disrespect happen? Why did it happen? How was John Wooden able to win 10 national championships in 12 years with players of outstanding character like Kareem? If Wooden were still coaching, he probably wouldn't put up with players like Allen Iverson. He probably would never recruit players like Allen Iverson in the first place. But the reality is, he probably wouldn't win any national titles without a few Iversons on his team. That's a dilemma any coach trying to do the right thing will face nowadays. Yes, the world has changed since Wooden coached. The difficulty of imagining John Wooden coaching today tells you how much it's changed. And the cultural currents are much too complex to pinpoint a single culprit.

But we agree with Simon in *Grand Canyon:* It doesn't have to be this way, and it's not supposed to be this way. What we've argued throughout this book is that a sports culture that is based on an understanding of sport *as sport* is, above all else, a culture of respect: respect for opponents, respect for teammates, respect for officials, respect for the game, and respect between coaches and players. We're not so naive as to think that coaches teaching sportsmanship will magically transform our entire culture into a culture of respect, but, given the pronounced parallels between the sports world and our general culture, it's certainly one place to make an effort to cultivate respect. The culture of disrespect should be addressed at all levels and in all of its many manifestations in our society, but one focal point should be sport.

> ## *Time-Out for Reflection*
>
> - Do you agree that there has been a decline in civility in our broader culture over the past few decades? Can you give examples of public discourse that is uncivil?
> - What is civility? Why does it matter? In effect, this book argues that civility and competitiveness are compatible in the sports world. Are they compatible in our general culture?
> - Would the cultivation of a culture of respect in the sports world contribute to a broader culture of respect? Are there ways to emphasize that connection?

Sport and Education

Despite the dreary aspects of highly commercialized sport, where money, hype, and celebrity dominate the broadcasts, the sports pages, and the Web sites, it's still possible to focus on the uncorrupted activities we played as we were growing up, we coach in our local venues, we teach to our children, and we continue to play as we age. At the heart of sport are values worth preserving and reinforcing. Given the widespread interest in sport and the extent to which children are involved in it, there are tremendous educational opportunities available for the development of habits and attitudes that may have a significant impact on a young person's life. If sports are played properly, if coaches and parents are able to conceptualize sport in ways that resist the corrupting influences of our big-money culture of celebrity and status, then sport participation may have a much better chance of fulfilling its promise as a locus of moral education.

There is a lively and interesting debate among scholars of sport concerning the basis for ethics in sport. Are ethical values in sport continuous with the central values of commonsense morality (benevolence, justice, honesty, generosity), or are they distinctive and internal to sport? Certainly some of the actions permitted or even required in sport would be ethically impermissible in ordinary life (for example, imagine blocking or tackling a fellow customer at the grocery store). Part of the problem with certain kinds of behaviors in contemporary sport seems to be connected with our sense that, unfortunately, we leave ordinary norms behind when we enter the sports world (for example, think about fan behavior at games or out-of-control parents attacking coaches or officials). Sometimes sport does allow what would otherwise be questionable behavior; sometimes we want to remind people of ordinary concerns about violence, aggression, and uncivil displays.

For our purposes, we need not resolve all of the knotty problems related to this dispute, nor do we have to adopt an exclusively internalist or externalist approach. The central argument of this book has been, broadly speaking, internalist. We have sought to ground the virtue of sportsmanship and the principles of respect in our description of the nature of the activity—that is, our sense that we can identify the uncorrupted essential features of sport. These features generate values that are at the heart of sports participation and should be the focus of the kind of moral education appropriate for engaging in sports. What are these values?

Sports are rule-governed activities, contests in which we come together with other persons, not in order to produce something, but simply to seek the goals internal to the activity, to overcome artificially constructed obstacles, to achieve a certain kind of excellence, and in doing so to participate in an inherently valuable activity. Rules apply equally to every participant, so equality is at the heart of sport. Playing by the rules isn't merely a contingent matter—it's essential to participating, since the cheater, in attempting to gain an unfair advantage in order to win, isn't really playing the game. Fair play is, in an important sense, simply playing, since the sport is defined by its central rules. The goal is not merely to win, in the sense of producing the winning score, but to do so *within the constraints of the rules* that define the sport.

The condition for the possibility of becoming better, achieving excellence, is competing with others in contests, so *your* competitive excellence depends on a cooperative structure in which a good opponent challenges you—and for which you ought to be thankful and grateful. In more formal settings, you should acknowledge the contributions of coaches, officials, and (where appropriate) teammates to your own quest for personal excellence and satisfying experiences. Insofar as sport involves the playing of games, the playful character of sport is appropriately acknowledged by a kind of generosity and graciousness in relating to opponents. Sport is not war; it's competitive *play*. Because success in sport is not easy and failure is inevitable, it takes hard work, perseverance, and courage to become better. Because success in sport depends on so many factors over which one has no control (innate physical ability, good coaches, caring parents, trustworthy teammates, luck in the game), the thrill of success or pride in victory ought to be combined with a profound sense of humility, which might serve to moderate our tendencies to be predominantly self-centered and egotistical.

We don't claim that this brief account of the internal values of sport provides an exhaustive list of such values, but it should be instructive. We have mentioned equality, fair play, cooperation, trust, gratitude, generosity, graciousness, perseverance, and humility. These are not alien values transported into the world of sport from elsewhere. They are *sport's own values*—and they should be taught as such. Competition *can* break down and produce alienation, but it need not and should not. Sport *can* be corrupted by a win-at-all-costs attitude often fueled by economic concerns and a particular view of social life, but such an attitude isn't essential to the uncorrupted thing in question. And, in fact, the old dictum that "sports build character" depends on the notion that sport participation can be beneficial, that the values internal to sport can become embodied as character traits that are firm and applicable in everyday life. If we are serious about the character-building aspects of sport, then we ought to focus on coaching for character, especially in our educational institutions.

In chapter 2, we pointed out that the English word "ethics" comes from the Greek word for habit, *ethos,* and that virtue, good character, can be viewed as deeply ingrained habits. For that reason, Aristotle says that the virtues—courage, self-control, and justice, for example—can be acquired by practicing them. Sport can build character because it offers an opportunity to practice the virtues, to practice good character. But of course that means it also offers an opportunity to practice the vices—rashness or recklessness instead of courage, emotional license instead of self-control, injustice instead of justice. It all depends on how we approach sport.

If we justify the millions of dollars we spend each year on school athletics with the claim that sport builds character, we need to approach school and youth athletics with that in mind. And, in spite of all of the external goods that stem from school athletics—community entertainment, school spirit, middle-aged men and women getting to relive their childhoods through their children—nothing could justify all of that investment unless there is an *educational* purpose to school athletics. Central to the educational purpose of youth athletics is the opportunity to practice and develop good character.

We should add one qualification, however. Not only can sport build bad character when conducted improperly, but in our experience the habits of sportsmanship that athletes develop on the playing field don't automatically carry over into the rest of their lives. Sometimes there's an odd disconnect. For many athletes the same deeply ingrained habits of respect—or deeply ingrained habits of disrespect—do manifest themselves on and off the field. Disrespectful jerks on the field are often disrespectful jerks off the field, and athletes who exhibit integrity and respect in their sports often are human beings of supreme character in their lives. But it also helps if coaches, parents, school administrators, journalists, and the athletes themselves try to make that connection explicitly. Coaches and parents need to teach young athletes that the good character they are developing on the playing field should carry over into their lives. Somewhat paradoxically, sport gives us an opportunity to practice virtue precisely when we focus on sport as sport, as opposed to sport as a workshop for life, but as educators we need to remind ourselves that the purpose of all education is to prepare young people for life as a whole.

Wrap-Up

In part III, we offer a broader perspective on sport. In this chapter we offered some reflections on the relation of sport to society and on the function of sport in education. Ironically, if we try to turn sport into a panacea that will solve all of society's ills, we will lose track of what is so special about sport—and we will diminish the ability of sports participation to actually make a contribution to broader social goals. But sports education can make a contribution—develop character, strike a blow for civility, stem the growing tide of disrespect that so many young people are attracted to.

In the final chapter, we will venture further beyond the walls of the stadiums and look at sport in relation not just to society but to life as a whole.

NINE

So, Callicles, I have been convinced by these accounts; it has become my concern how I may present to the judge my soul in its healthiest condition. I relinquish, therefore, the honors that most men pursue and shall endeavor, by cultivating the truth, to be as good as I may during my life and, when I come to die, in my dying. And insofar as I am able I urge all other men (and you in particular I summon, thus countering your former summons to me) to such a life and such a contest as this, which I affirm to be worth all the contests here on earth put together.

~ Plato, The Gorgias (Helmbold translation)

Beyond Sport

At the beginning of part I, we invited you to become more reflective about your own experience. But becoming more reflective about your own experience inevitably means going beyond your own experience in order to gain perspective on it. In this case, that means thinking about the nature of athletic competition in a more theoretical way than you ordinarily do in the day-to-day activities of an athletic coach. You ought to embody an understanding of the nature of athletic competition when you make split-second decisions during a game or a practice, but you won't be consciously reflecting on it. In order to embody that understanding, however, you do have to think about it, reflect on it, pay attention to what others have thought and said about it. As an educator, you do need to set aside time to become more reflective about what you do—and you will do a better job at what you do if you become more reflective about it.

In this chapter, we invite you to think back on some of the broader themes that we've repeatedly touched on throughout the book and to relate those themes to some of the broader ethical and philosophical issues that we have not dealt with. In chapter 8, we asked you to think about sport and society. Now we invite you to think about the relation between sport and life, or, rather, sport and life as a whole. As we intimated in chapter 2, underlying the two extreme views of sport are equally extreme views about what life is all about. Thinking about sport, just like thinking about any serious human endeavor, inevitably leads us to think about the relation between that endeavor and life as a whole.

What we've said so far makes a lot of sense without these connections, but we'd like to leave you with some final thoughts on the relation between sport and life. In "Putting Sport in Perspective," we'll reiterate one of the recurring themes of the book, the need to recognize that sport is not the whole of life, and in "Reconnecting Sport and Life," we'll make some suggestions for understanding how sport is, nonetheless, connected to the whole of life—and even how sport is very much "about" life.

We won't provide a series of answers, but we will try to leave you with a sense of the abiding question of human existence: How ought I to live my life? Becoming reflective about sport ultimately means becoming reflective about life. Parts I and II by themselves can help you understand the principles of sportsmanship that you should embody and teach in your coaching, but here we invite you to go one step further and think about how what you do is related to the most basic human questions.

Putting Sport in Perspective

One of the most important themes that we have developed in this book concerns perspective. Of course, in one obvious sense the only way we can see things is from where we are. But it is a remarkable fact of human experience that we have the capacity to see things so differently *from where we are.* We inevitably use spatial metaphors here. We can see things "narrowly" or "broadly," we can be "closed-minded" or we can "enlarge" our vision, our point of view can be "cramped" and "limited," but we even have the capacity to consider how things might look from God's perspective, *sub specie aeternitatis.* We are finite beings, spatially and temporally, but our minds roam over infinity. In one context, we think of our true selves as what's "inside"—especially when we talk about feelings and emotions. But, in another context, we lose track of any sense of the "inside," and we focus our attention on something "outside" ourselves—the catcher's mitt, a beautiful mountain, another person. In fact, when we describe our *experience,* it's not at all clear that the concepts of inside and outside make sense at all.

Our perspective on the world is always limited, but it's often broader than we give ourselves credit for, and often it could become broader than our egos would have us believe. Often the only way to understand and appreciate what is closest to us is to cast our glance away from it in order to see it against a wider background. And when we do this, something happens to us. Because we see more broadly, we see more. We compare, we inevitably make judgments, and when we return to the object of our original attention, our focus has been reshaped.

As we have suggested, good sportsmanship requires understanding and practice. When we appreciate the wonderful complexity of sport participation, including the essential roles played by opponents, teammates, coaches, and officials, as well as the rich traditions and customs of the various games, our attitudes are changed, our spirit is enlarged. The limited desires of the egoistic self are transformed into the respectful concerns of a more substantial self whose character has developed and whose actions attest to this. By seeing ourselves as part of a greater whole, we are enriched by it. But if it is important to turn our respectful gaze toward our fellow participants *within* the world of sport, it is perhaps even more important, from the standpoint of our fundamental attitudes and the development of character, to turn our reflective attention away from sport to the whole of life. We need perspective on sport itself.

"It's Only a Game"

As we have argued, participation in sport can play an important role in the moral education of young people, if not by explicit instruction then at least by the habits it can instill. The game, however, has the power not only to uplift and encourage, it can also depress and ultimately destroy—if it is not kept in perspective. Consider the sad case of a former major league pitcher whose life spiraled downward and ended in suicide after he gave up the big homer in the play-offs. There is a monumental difference between playing the game *as if* it were the only thing in the world that mattered and truly believing it *is* the only thing in the world that matters. Coaches have a tremendous responsibility in this regard. As motivators, they must get their players to play as if each game, each inning, each pitch were indeed the only thing in the universe that mattered; as educators in the broader sense, they must figure out how to do this in such a way that they never let their players forget that no pitch, no inning, no game, is—pardon the sports metaphor—the whole ball game. Or, to use the standard expression, "It's only a game."

Perhaps it's a cliché or such an obvious truism that its outward expression seems unneeded, but sometimes wisdom is nothing other than internalizing and living the truth of the truism. And that requires that we think about the truism, for the truth of a truism is not the simple fact that it states, but the perspective it calls for. Truisms ask us to see things in light of something so obvious we often ignore it. "Man cannot live by bread alone," "Everyone must die," "It's only a game." Everybody knows it's only a game, but we need to state the obvious because it's easy to become so absorbed in the game that we forget the obvious. To live the truth of the truism that it's only a game is to come to appreciate how sport fits into the whole of life, where the true value of sport resides, and how to integrate the love of the game and the pursuit of athletic excellence into a life lived well. It means putting sport within the proper perspective and maintaining the proper balance of seriousness and playfulness that a broader perspective calls for. Coaches, parents, and educators must communicate this truism not by mindlessly stating it or posting it on the locker-room wall but with all their actions and all their words.

As we write, and as coaches all over the United States tell young athletes that winning this game is the only thing that matters, there are children who are living and dying in such abysmal circumstances that they have never had the opportunity to play an organized game of any kind. In a world in which hunger, disease, suffering, and violence confront us daily, the value of devoting our attention to playing athletic games should be affirmed with some degree of modesty. The internal goals of sports—throwing a slow curveball well, shooting an arrow into the 10 ring at 90 meters in a strong crosswind, hitting a perfect touch volley—seem trivial by comparison. Athletic games can be exuberant, intensely absorbing, joyful, but, at its best, sport is *splendid triviality*. To say that sport is splendid triviality is to acknowledge its modest place in the scale of significant human concerns. Nor is sport the only human practice that offers so much to its participants and fans. Certainly there are other practices—music, art, mathematics—that can be just as demanding, as rich, as educational, and, in their own way, as joyful as sport. Turning our attention away from our immediate concern with sport and toward the whole of life should produce another kind of humility, one that wisely recognizes the smallness of our athletic concerns in the face of the largeness of life. Coaches, parents, teachers, and everyone else who is involved in the moral education of young athletes need to remind them how lucky they are to be able to *play*, to be able to pursue this unique kind of excellence for at least a small part of their lives.

Time-Out for Reflection

- What are some of the positive events that can happen in a person's life that would be more important than winning a game? What are some of the tragedies that can happen in a person's life that would be more important than losing a game?

- If sport is "splendid triviality," can you think of aspects of life that are the opposite—crucial and necessary drudgery?

- How could you explain the "as if" notion of playing sports to youth athletes in a way that would make sense to them?

Winners and Losers in Life?

From the standpoint of this broader perspective, some of the facile analogies between sport and life that tend to blow up the athletic arena until it encompasses everything lose their legitimacy. Yes, life is like a baseball game (or, as one of our friends ironically put it, life is a metaphor for baseball)—but in what respects? Too often the sport–life analogy develops a life of its own and becomes an answer to every question, a cure for every ill. If we situate sport within the context of the whole of life, we might well "live the truth of the truisms" about sport and life, but there is a corresponding danger that we will let the endless slogans, clichés, and analogies do our thinking for us. Some truisms state the obvious in order to give us perspective, some slogans and analogies overstate the case to make a point, and some slogans and analogies, because of their rhetorical punch, trick us into accepting a view of sport and life that we might otherwise see through.

Two examples: "Winning isn't everything; it's the only thing" and "Show me a good loser and I'll show you a loser." As rhetorical devices designed to get players to walk on the field in order to play as if this game is the only thing that matters, to help them avoid the trap of walking on the field prepared to lose, these slogans may serve a legitimate purpose. But all too often we take them, or even consciously intend for them, to mean that, literally, sport and life are about winning and nothing else. Then we end up with school board members claiming that a losing season teaches the players to be "losers in life" or a winning season teaches them to be "winners in life," a claim that misconstrues both the nature of sport and the nature of life. There are indeed winners in sport, but is there really such a thing as a winner in life? If one side wins in sport, the other side necessarily loses. If I am a winner in life, would I then cause someone else to be a loser? That analogy might make sense in the business world—if I make a lot of money, someone else will make less—but if I live the best life I am capable of living, if I am the best person I am capable of being, do I cause others to live worse lives, to be worse human beings? On the contrary, as we have already discussed, my living well—that is, living ethically well—will enhance the lives of those around me.

Of course, when we thought more deeply about the nature of competitive sport, we found that sport, in the end, is not about winning either, but about the mutual striving for excellence. Interestingly enough, John Wooden even resorted to the metaphorical use of winning to say what he thought was truly important in sport: "I believe we have 'won'—that is, accomplished all we're capable of accomplishing—when we've *lost* games" (Walton, p. 67). Wooden, having thought deeply about sport and about life, kept the metaphor in its proper place by quickly explaining what he really meant by the word "won." In other words, it isn't really the winning in sport that ought to serve as a model for life but the excellence we achieve in doing our best to win. The athletic experience can no more be reduced to the winning-is-everything cliché than life can be reduced to looking out for number one in a dog-eat-dog world. Life is about being tough enough to stand up to enemies when we ought to stand up to them, tough enough to walk away when we ought to walk away, and tough enough to cultivate friendships, to contribute to the excellence of others, even occasionally to make friends of enemies. Some have even argued that life requires the moral courage to love our enemies.

Reconnecting Sport and Life

Even if sport isn't everything, it's surely something, and if we're right about what we've said in this book, it can be an important thing at that. Sport is separate from the rest of life—it takes place in special places marked off from the rest of the world. But these special places and the games we play in them have more to do with the rest of our lives than this separation might suggest.

The Virtue of Sportsmanship and the Virtues of a Life Lived Well

As we have argued, sport provides an arena in which good character can be developed and practiced. Sport is surely not the only arena in which young people can learn to be persistent, determined, respectful, trustworthy, courageous, responsible, fair, and honest. If young people devote themselves to any practices in which there are standards of excellence, traditions, and learned teachers, such virtues can be developed. Young violinists as well as young gymnasts have an opportunity to practice virtue. But sport is important and pervasive in our lives. In sport we have ample opportunities to help young people become the kind of people who will not only be successful and respected in the world of sport but in life as well. And even the more mature members of the sports world—coaches, administrators, and parents—will have significant and unique moral challenges to confront as they respond to the tensions and dramatic resonances of competitive athletics. Sport may not be everything, but it can have real existential bite.

Sport and life are connected, not because there are winners and losers in life, but because good character matters in both. In the *Nicomachean Ethics,* Aristotle described the goal of a human life this way: "We reach the conclusion that the good of man is an activity of the soul in conformity with excellence or virtue, and if there are several virtues, with the best and most complete" (p. 17). In that sense, moral education in athletics—that is, education in excellence of character—can prepare young people for life. Courage, discipline, fairness—simply put, these are good things.

Sport and the Virtues of the Mind

Our extended comments on sport and character in this book have hardly exhausted the subject. We have articulated and defended various principles of sportsmanship, but our comments have also served to raise important questions. We are convinced that questions about sport and character should be raised by all coaches in order to promote reflection on the part of the players. To make the right choices in light of principles of sportsmanship requires experience and good judgment. It may be obvious to most thoughtful people that sport can promote the growth of certain character traits. In particular, sport can emphasize virtues of character such as courage and responsibility. But what about the traits that will come into play when athletes—and especially coaches and administrators—have to address fundamental questions about what they are doing, how they are to act, and how they stand in relation to life as a whole? It's not at all clear that sport, in and of itself, promotes the intellectual virtues of critical thinking. Sport is competitive *physical* play. Yet moral education in the full sense of the word is not mindless moral indoctrination or even the unreflective inculcation of values. Moral wisdom requires experience, deliberation, and good judgment. Moral education in its full sense requires the development of good thinking along with good character, a good head along with a good heart.

So why shouldn't you ask questions and invite players to *reflect,* not simply to be obedient? Why shouldn't you challenge players to question themselves? Why shouldn't you show players that it is important to thoughtfully engage in sport? As athletes we all yearn for the "unconsciousness" of a great streak, but as full human beings, we should aspire to the kind of thoughtful reflection that enables us to *understand* why the experience of a streak is so uplifting, what it means to say it is "unconscious," and why this sort of experience has to be situated within a whole life lived well. Socratic questioning is generally inappropriate in the middle of a basketball game (although Socratic irony might sometimes be advisable in disagreeing with an official), but there is no reason why coaches and teachers can't teach student-athletes to reflect—at least after the game is over—about the meaning of their experiences on the court or playing field. In other words, in order to make the connection between sport and life meaningful, we may need to cultivate virtues of the mind that athletic experience itself may not naturally promote.

Time–Out for Reflection

- What would you say are chief characteristics of a "life lived well"? In other words, what really matters in life? Or, in Aristotle's terms, what is "the good for a human"?

- Some theories of life contend that you can live life "in the zone"—that is, without thinking. If you find the right "balance," or "center," or "peace of mind," everything will fall into place automatically. Can you think of situations in life or aspects of life that require thoughtful reflection or careful deliberation?

- What are some specific ways to emphasize the importance of the virtues of the mind in athletics?

Sport: Escape or Revelation?

When we start to *think* about sport, we recognize that character development does not exhaust the meaning that sport has for us. We have repeatedly referred to the exhilaration, the beauty, of the game. Indeed, there may be a further relation between sport and life that bears some thought. Or is there? Some critics, and even some defenders, claim that sport is an escape from the realities of everyday life. The critics say it is a delusionary escape from real life; the defenders say it takes us away from the injustice and toil of the work world, that it creates an ideal space in which the good triumph and the bad lose. There's probably some truth in both of these views: Sport does create a separate world, take us out of the everyday, the ordinary, the workaday. It has a beauty all its own. The exhilaration, then, seems to come not from a connection between sport and life but from their separateness.

But the separateness of our fields of dreams, like the separateness of our actual dreams, can be misleading. One doesn't have to accept the full-blown apparatus of Freudian psychoanalysis to recognize that dreams often reflect the deeper concerns of our waking lives. Perhaps a better analogy—one that is not commonly made—might be between sport and art. We speak of the art world much as we speak of the sports world—the world of art is a world of its own, and the works of art produced in it create their own worlds. Works of art are creations out of nothing, fictions, products of the imagination. In fact, many philosophers have identified art as a form of play.

But this characterization can be misleading. For great art, and even not-so-great art, takes us out of the everyday, the ordinary, creates a separate world of its own—but ultimately reflects back upon the whole of life. We come away from an inspired performance of a Bach concerto, a made-up arrangement of sounds, with a sense of transcendence, a sense of how the harmony of seemingly discordant strands is at the heart of all things. We come away from Faulkner's fictitious Yoknapatawpha County with a sense of the power of past and place, a deeper sense of what it means to be human. We come away from van Gogh's swirling distortions in *Starry Night* with a deeper understanding of the emotions we all feel in the face of the swirling vastness of the universe. The separateness of an artwork opens up a special space in which we come to see things about ourselves and the world that we could not otherwise see. On one level, art appears to be an escape from reality; on another, it reveals it, reflects it, even enriches it. The purpose of dramatic "playing," says Hamlet, "both at the first and now, was and is to hold, as 'twere, the mirror up to nature; to show virtue her own feature, scorn her own image, and the very age and body of the time his form and pressure" (III. ii).

We suggest that sport, like art, holds so much meaning for us because, at some deeper level that is difficult to articulate, it too reflects back on the whole of life. If we're thoughtful in how we teach particular sports, if we're dedicated and conscientious, and if we're graced with good luck, we may have experiences in sport that put us in touch with some of the deeper realities of life. Sport, like art, may appear to be a mere escape from reality—and, let's be honest, it very often does function as just that—but it can provide a special mirror for it, a stage for its presentation, an open space in which some very important things can show themselves.

From this perspective, it may well be possible to raise again the notion that life is a kind of game, or at least a form of play. As an invitation to pursue some of these questions and to use athletic experience as a springboard for this reflection, we'll mention a few of the thoughts on this subject that we've developed more fully elsewhere. The view you hold of life—for example, do you think of life as fundamentally a matter of work or play?—will affect the view you have of sport. If life is fundamentally work, then play isn't an opportunity for revelation but rather a mere escape from the reality of work. But, by the same token, the experiences we have in playing seriously may well reflect on how we view life. Johan Huizinga suggests that humans are essentially *playing* creatures, and more than one philosopher has suggested that life might well be understood as dead-serious play. It's reasonable to say that life ought to be lived as if it mattered absolutely, even though in some ultimate sense none of us knows if it really matters. Of course, the as-if quality of a ball game comes in part from the fact that we know there will be other games and other experiences in life, whereas we have only one life to live. The as-if quality of the play of life, then, has a different character. On the one hand, when we say that someone treats life as a game or is playing at life, we mean to say that this person doesn't take it seriously enough. On the other hand, we often need to remind others or ourselves to lighten up, to keep a sense of humor, to appreciate the ironic character of life. Is the balance of playfulness and seriousness we articulated in our discussion of sport the same balance we ought to seek in life?

It's worth mentioning here that thinking about the nature of play has even led some philosophers and theologians not merely beyond the ballpark and the art gallery, but even beyond the questions about the place of play in a human life. We can and often do draw facile, self-serving analogies between sport and life, and as we broaden the spheres of play, the possibility of making connections too quickly and too easily increases. Nonetheless, if we think about sport as a form of play—that is, as an activity that has no purpose beyond itself—we might well come to wonder not just whether human life is in some fundamental sense a matter of play, but whether reality in general doesn't have something of this character. Friedrich Schlegel wrote, "All the sacred games of art are only remote imitations of the infinite play of the world, the eternally self-creating work of art" (Gadamer 1993, p. 101). Isn't it possible to ask the same question about the sacred games of sport?

If play is a purely human phenomenon, something we make up, then all of the other references we make to play—the play of waves in the ocean, the wind playing tricks with us, the play of light on the water, the "infinite play of the world"—would be metaphorical. Those things don't *really,* literally play; we simply see them in light of human experience. Some thinkers, however, have suggested that the self-renewal of nature, its effortless playing of itself without any purpose beyond itself, might well be the "literal" sense of play. That play feels so "natural" to us might well come from deeper sources in us than we realize. Play, then, far from being an escape from reality may be an expression of it. Of course, we don't ordinarily think about these things as we are playing sports, but it may well be that it is precisely because of these deeper connections that we feel, in a way that's difficult to articulate, most "real" when we play.

Time-Out for Reflection

- Think of a work of art you find beautiful—a painting, a musical work, a play, a literary work—and try to articulate what makes it beautiful. Then think of your favorite sport and try to articulate what is beautiful about it.
- What do you consider the "deeper realities of life"? What aspects of sport hold a mirror up to those realities?
- Does the claim that life is "dead-serious play" conflict with the values of the Protestant work ethic? If the overall framework of life is play, how does work fit into that framework?

Wrap-Up

While all of the other chapters of this book achieve some kind of closure, we mean for this chapter to open out into, to point to, what we haven't fully discussed. Underlying the closure of the previous chapters is an arena and a tradition of philosophical reflection that we have only touched upon here, and we hope that these musings might serve as an invitation to spend more time in this arena. The charge of juvenile escapism has been leveled at philosophy as well—and sometimes with good reason—but we contend that the step back of good thinking, like the seeming artificiality of art and sport, can ultimately put us in touch with the things that truly matter. And when Socrates said the unexamined life is not worth living for a human being, he did not exclude coaches or athletes.

BIBLIOGRAPHY

In order not to break up the text with scholarly citations, we have avoided the mechanisms of scholarly citation as much as possible. We have, however, depended heavily on certain sources, in some cases directly quoting and in others not, so it is appropriate to give credit where credit is due. Second, we would like to give some indication of the background that informs this book. The conciseness and clarity we've achieved in articulating the principles of sportsmanship derive in part from our experience as coaches and athletes, but in large part from our philosophical backgrounds. Some of these sources we refer to explicitly in the text of our book, and others are listed here because they have informed our thinking in a significant way. Finally, in the event that someone might want to pursue some of these topics in a more scholarly fashion, we wanted to use this opportunity to suggest additional readings.

For these reasons, our list of bibliographical entries is preceded by a short bibliographical essay explaining the most significant sources that have informed our thinking on the subject of sportsmanship. We will first say a few words about some of the more significant influences on our thinking; then we'll provide a more complete list of relevant readings and sources.

Our view of sport as a form of play has been influenced by various writers who have written about play. *Homo Ludens: A Study of the Play Element in Culture*, by Johan Huizinga, is perhaps *the* seminal study of play and its relation to various expressions of human culture—language, law, war, poetry, etc. The first chapter contains an important analysis of the concept of play. Kenneth Schmitz's "Sport and Play: Suspension of the Ordinary" is one of the most concise applications of Huizinga's concept of play to the arena of sport, and our treatment of the nature of sport in chapter 2 follows his thinking very closely. In his *Truth and Method*, the great German philosopher Hans-Georg Gadamer puts forward the view that art is a form of play. Although he only briefly discusses sport and games, his account helps to clarify the way in which both art and sport are forms of a fundamental aspect of being human, perhaps even a fundamental aspect of nature. We touch briefly on this broader approach to the concept of play in chapter 9.

For obvious reasons, our emphasis on achieving a balance between playfulness and seriousness in sport and sportsmanship closely follows chapters 4 through 6 of Randolph Feezell's *Sport, Play, and Ethical Reflection*. Also, Craig Clifford's dialogue "Coach" in *The Tenure of Phil Wisdom* treats many of the ideas that we've developed in this book, and some of the discussion was modeled from passages in this dialogue. Our view of competition has been strongly influenced by Drew Hyland's account in his article "Competition and Friendship," as well as chapter 2 of his book, *Philosophy of Sport*. The idea that competition is a "mutual striving for excellence" we take from Hyland.

Another great German philosopher, Martin Heidegger (Gadamer's teacher), has been a significant influence. His book, *Being and Time,* contains one of the most profound reflections on the nature of human existence in the history of philosophy. In particular, our emphasis on understanding human finitude derives in large part from Heidegger's thought. His understanding of human "authenticity" in terms of seeing one's true possibilities is particularly pertinent. Iris Murdoch's essay, "The Sovereignty of Good Over Other Concepts," parallels Heidegger's call for a truthful coming to terms with our own finitude. Murdoch connects the development of virtue, or moral excellence, with coming to see the world as it is; that is, she relates the possibility of making ourselves better with a kind of truthful vision of the world, what she calls attaining a "just mode of vision." She also interprets humility in terms of "seeing the way things are." This concept is crucial to our understanding of sportsmanship, and we make reference to it throughout the book.

Our treatment of virtue as excellence of character is, of course, indebted to the classical Greek tradition of moral philosophy, expressed most profoundly in many of Plato's dialogues and in Aristotle's *Nicomachean Ethics*. The role of good judgment (*phronēsis*) in relation to the development of good character is famously emphasized by Aristotle in book VI of his *Ethics*. Randolph Feezell's "Sport, Character, and Virtue," chapter 9 in *Sport, Play, and Ethical Reflection,* shows the way in which various virtues might be developed through participation in sports. Feezell's chapter and, in general, our understanding of the relation between virtue and sport are heavily influenced by Alasdair MacIntyre's widely discussed book, *After Virtue.* This important work in moral philosophy first situates the virtues in the context of what MacIntyre calls "practices." One distinguishing characteristic of a practice, according to MacIntyre, is that it is a human activity that involves standards of excellence. You can do it well or poorly. Baseball or football or any sport would be a practice; so would playing the violin. MacIntyre distinguishes the internal goods of a practice (in baseball that would include hitting a good line drive) from the external goods that participation in a practice may bring about (fame and fortune, for example). He emphasizes that the internal goods are in some sense shared by participants in the practice (developing a more intelligent all-court game after seeing Roger Federer play tennis), unlike the external goods that are in principle scarce (fame and fortune).

Also, our emphasis on the historical nature of sport follows MacIntyre's emphasis on the way practices are constituted by their traditions. A more in-depth account of our thinking about the importance of custom and tradition for understanding the issue of cheating in sports is found in Randolph Feezell's "On Cheating in Sports," chapter 7 of *Sport, Play, and Ethical Reflection*. In this essay, cheating is understood as taking an unfair advantage of an opponent. It might involve explicit rules, but it might also be a matter of failing to respect the customs and traditions that all participants of the game have implicitly agreed to abide by.

Our view of the function of rules and the role of officials is, not surprisingly, described in the familiar language of Thomas Hobbes. In chapter XIII of *Leviathan*, Hobbes describes a hypothetical situation, which he calls the "state of war," in which people live prior to the development of moral constraints. We've found his description of the state of war helpful in trying to understand what sports would become after the dissolution of moral constraints—assuming, for the purposes of argument, that that has not already occurred.

In chapter 6 of *The Culture of Narcissism*, Christopher Lasch provides an interesting commentary on the "Degradation of Sport" and the trivialization of sport and athletics in contemporary culture. He speaks of sport as "splendid futility." Since he emphasizes the playful character of sport, he might well have agreed with our characterization of sport as "splendid triviality."

In chapter 8, our view of sports heroes and role models reflects some of the thinking found in Randolph Feezell's "Celebrated Athletes, Moral Exemplars, and Lusory Objects." And, finally, our comments on wisdom and truisms in chapter 9 have been influenced by Stanley Godlovitch's essay "On Wisdom."

Aristotle. *Nicomachean Ethics*. Translated by Martin Ostwald. Indianapolis: Bobbs-Merrill (Library of Liberal Arts), 1962.

Bennett, William J. *The Book of Virtues: A Treasury of Great Moral Stories*. New York: Simon and Schuster, 1993.

Blackburn, Simon. *Being Good: A Short Introduction to Ethics*. New York: Oxford University Press, 2001.

Bradley, Bill. *Life on the Run*. New York: Vintage Books, 1976.

Clifford, Craig. "Temper-Tantruming: The Immoral Implications of Tennis." *Fort Worth Star-Telegram*, 22 July 1985 (also appeared in *Baltimore Sun*, 11 August 1985).

———. "Whatever the Goal in Life or Sports, Winning Is More Than Highest Score." *Fort Worth Star-Telegram*, 3 April 1988 (also appeared in *San Diego Tribune*, 8 April 1988).

———. "Coach." In *The Tenure of Phil Wisdom: Dialogues*. Lanham, MD: University Press of America, 1995.

Dent, Jim. *The Undefeated: The Oklahoma Sooners and the Greatest Winning Streak in College Football*. New York: Thomas Dunne Books, 2001.

Feezell, Randolph. *Sport, Play, and Ethical Reflection*. Urbana, IL: University of Illinois Press, 2004.

———. "Celebrated Athletes, Moral Exemplars, and Lusory Objects." *Journal of the Philosophy of Sport 32*, no. 1 (2005).

Ford, Gerald. "In Defense of the Competitive Urge." In *Sport Inside Out: Readings in Literature and Philosophy*, edited by David L. Vanderwerden and Spencer K. Wertz. Fort Worth: Texas Christian University Press, 1985.

Gadamer, Hans-Georg. *Truth and Method*. Translated by Joel Weinsheimer and Donald G. Marshall. New York: Continuum, 1993.

Grand Canyon. Directed by Lawrence Kasdan. Los Angeles: Twentieth Century-Fox, 1991.

Hayes, Graham. April 28, 2008. "Central Washington Offers the Ultimate Act of Sportsmanship." espn.com.

Heckathorn, Douglas D. "Collective Sanctions and Compliance Norms: A Formal Theory of Group-Mediated Social Control." *American Sociological Review* 55 (1990): 366–384.

Heidegger, Martin. *Being and Time*. Translated by John Macquarrie and Edward Robinson. New York: Harper and Row, 1962.

Heinegg, Peter. "Philosopher in the Playground: Notes on the Meaning of Sport." In *Sport Inside Out: Readings in Literature and Philosophy,* edited by David L. Vanderwerden and Spencer K. Wertz. Fort Worth: Texas Christian University Press, 1985.

Herrigel, Eugen. *Zen in the Art of Archery*. Translated by R.R.C. Hull. New York: Vintage Books, 1971.

Hobbes, Thomas. *Leviathan*. In *Classics of Western Philosophy,* 4th edition, edited by Steven M. Cahn. Indianapolis: Hackett, 1995.

Huizinga, Johan. *Homo Ludens: A Study of the Play-Element in Culture*. Boston: Beacon Press, 1950.

Hyland, Drew A. "Competition and Friendship." *Journal of the Philosophy of Sport* V (1978).

———. *Philosophy of Sport*. New York: Paragon House, 1990.

Jackson, Phil. *Sacred Hoops*. New York: Hyperion, 1995.

Kant, Immanuel. *Grounding for the Metaphysics of Morals*. Translated by James W. Ellington. 3rd edition. Indianapolis: Hackett, 1993.

Lasch, Christopher. *The Culture of Narcissism: American Life in an Age of Diminished Expectations*. New York: Warner Books, 1979.

Lipsyte, Robert. "The Emasculation of American Sports." *New York Times Magazine* (April 2, 1995).

MacIntyre, Alasdair. *After Virtue: A Study in Moral Theory*. South Bend, IN: University of Notre Dame Press, 1981.

Maclean, Norman. *A River Runs Through It and Other Stories*. Chicago: University of Chicago Press, 1976.

McGinn, Colin. *Sport*. Stocksfield, UK: Acumen, 2008.

Mitchell, George J. *Report to the Commissioner of Baseball of an Independent Investigation into the Illegal Use of Steroids and Other Performance Enhancing Substances by Players in Major League Baseball*. Commissioner of Baseball, December 13, 2007.

Morgan, William J., and Klaus V. Meier. *Philosophic Inquiry in Sport*. Champaign, IL: Human Kinetics, 1988.

Murdoch, Iris. "The Sovereignty of Good Over Other Concepts." In *The Sovereignty of Good*. New York: Schocken Books, 1971.

Plato. *The Collected Works of Plato*. Edited by Edith Hamilton and Huntington Cairns. Princeton, NJ: Princeton University Press, 1961.

Roberts, Randy, and James S. Olson. *Winning Is the Only Thing: Sports in America since 1945*. Baltimore: Johns Hopkins University Press, 1989.

Schmitz, Kenneth. "Sport and Play: Suspension of the Ordinary." *Philosophic Inquiry in Sport*. Champaign, IL: Human Kinetics, 1988.

Shakespeare, William. *The Tragedy of Hamlet, Prince of Denmark*. Heritage Shakespeare. Edited by Peter Alexander. New York: Heritage Press, 1958.

Verducci, Tom. "Baseball's Best." *Sports Illustrated* (May 1, 1995).

Walton, Gary M. Beyond Winning: The Timeless Wisdom of Great Philosopher Coaches. Champaign, IL: Leisure Press, 1992.

Wellman, Christopher. "Do Celebrated Athletes Have Special Responsibilities to Be Good Role Models? An Imagined Dialog Between Charles Barkley and Karl Malone." In *Sports Ethics: An Anthology,* edited by Jan Boxill. Malden, MA: Blackwell, 2003.

Will, George F. *Men at Work: The Craft of Baseball.* New York: HarperCollins, 1990.

ABOUT THE AUTHORS

CRAIG CLIFFORD is professor of philosophy and director of the honors programs at Tarleton State University in Stephenville, Texas.

Clifford received a PhD in philosophy from the State University of New York at Buffalo in 1981. He has an extensive background in teaching ethics and philosophy of sport, both at the undergraduate and graduate level.

A frequent guest columnist for several major newspapers, Clifford has frequently written on the subject of sportsmanship and the American sports culture. He is also the author of *Learned Ignorance in the Medicine Bow Mountains: A Reflection on Intellectual Prejudice* (Rodopi, 2008), *The Tenure of Phil Wisdom: Dialogues* (University Press of America, 1995), and *In the Deep Heart's Core: Reflections on Life, Letters, and Texas* (Texas A&M University Press, 1985).

From 1988 to 1992 Clifford coached the men's and women's tennis teams at Tarleton State University. He has competed in a number of sports. Taking up the sport of Olympic-style target archery in his mid-40s, he won the state outdoor archery championship in 1997 and finished the 1999 season ranked 26th in the nation.

RANDOLPH FEEZELL is professor of philosophy at Creighton University in Omaha, Nebraska.

Feezell received a PhD in philosophy from the State University of New York at Buffalo in 1977. He is an award-winning teacher at Creighton University; his classroom and research interests include ethics, philosophy of religion, and philosophy of sport. He is a member of the editorial board of the *Journal of the Philosophy of Sport*.

Feezell is the author of *Sport, Play, and Ethical Reflection* (University of Illinois Press, 2004) and *Faith, Freedom, and Value: Introductory Philosophical Dialogues* (Westview Press, 1989). He is the coauthor, with Curtis Hancock, of *How Should I Live? Philosophical Conversations About Moral Life* (Paragon House, 1991). He has also published numerous articles and reviews.

Feezell played baseball at the University of Oklahoma. He has coached baseball at virtually all levels, including over 10 years as a college assistant and hitting coach. He has played semiprofessional baseball, AAU basketball, and tournament tennis.